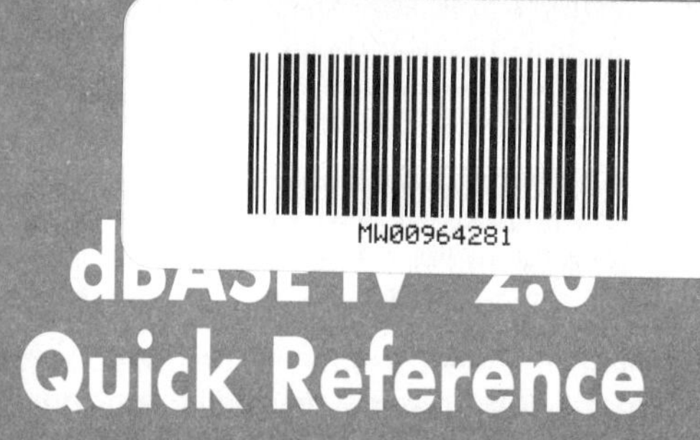

dBASE IV 2.0 Quick Reference

Que Quick Reference Series

STEVE DAVIS

dBASE IV 2.0 Quick Reference

Library of Congress Catalog Number: 93-84122

ISBN: 1-56529-267-7

96 95 94 93 4 3 2 1

Interpretation of the printing code: the rightmost double-digit number is the year of the book's printing; the rightmost single-digit number is the number of the book's printing. For example, a printing code of 93-4 shows that the fourth printing of the book occurred in 1993.

CREDITS

Publisher
David P. Ewing

Associate Publisher
Rick Ranucci

Operations Manager
Sheila Cunningham

Title Manager
Don Roche

Acquisitions Editor
Sarah Browning

Product Director
Robin Drake

Production Editor
Jill D. Bond

Technical Editor
Michael Watson

Production Team
Claudia Bell, Laurie Casey, Linda Koopman, Bob LaRoche, Caroline Roop, Sandra Shay

TRADEMARK ACKNOWLEDGMENTS

TABLE OF CONTENTS

COMMAND REFERENCE 1

= 1
?/?? 1
??? 2
! 3
*/&& 3
@...SAY/GET 3
@...TO/FILL/CLEAR/SCROLL 6
@...CLEAR/SCROLL 7
ACCEPT 7
ACTIVATE MENU 8
ACTIVATE POPUP 8
ACTIVATE SCREEN 8
ACTIVATE WINDOW 9
APPEND 9
APPEND FROM 10
APPEND MEMO 11
ASSIST 13
AVERAGE 13
BEGIN/END TRANSACTION 13
BLANK 14
BROWSE 15
CALCULATE/AVERAGE/SUM 18
CALL 19
CANCEL 20
CHANGE 21
CLEAR 21
CLOSE 22
COMPILE 23
CONTINUE 24
CONVERT 24
COPY 25

COUNT 26
CREATE APPLICATION 27
CREATE FROM 27
CREATE/MODIFY LABEL 28
CREATE/MODIFY QUERY/VIEW 29
CREATE/MODIFY REPORT 30
CREATE/MODIFY SCREEN 31
CREATE or MODIFY STRUCTURE 32
DEACTIVATE MENU 34
DEACTIVATE POPUP 34
DEACTIVATE WINDOW 34
DEBUG 34
DECLARE 35
DEFINE BAR 36
DEFINE BOX 36
DEFINE MENU/DEFINE PAD 37
DEFINE POPUP 38
DEFINE WINDOW 39
DELETE/PACK 41
DELETE FILE 42
DELETE TAG 42
DEXPORT 43
DIR 44
DISPLAY 45
DO 45
DO CASE/ENDCASE 46
DO WHILE/ENDDO 47
EDIT/CHANGE 48
EJECT/EJECT PAGE 50
ERASE 51
EXPORT 52
FIND 53
FUNCTION 55
GO/GOTO 56
HELP 57
IF/ENDIF 58
IMPORT 59
INDEX/REINDEX 60
INPUT 61
INSERT 62
JOIN 63

KEYBOARD 65
LABEL FORM 65
LIST/DISPLAY 66
LOAD 68
LOCATE 68
LOGOUT 69
MODIFY APPLICATION 70
MODIFY COMMAND/FILE 70
MODIFY LABEL 71
MODIFY QUERY/VIEW 71
MODIFY REPORT 71
MODIFY SCREEN 71
MODIFY STRUCTURE 72
MOVE WINDOW 72
NOTE 72
ON ERROR/ESCAPE/KEY 73
ON EXIT BAR/MENU/PAD/POPUP 74
ON MENU/POPUP 74
ON MOUSE 75
ON PAD 75
ON PAGE 76
ON READERROR 77
ON SELECTION BAR 77
ON SELECTION MENU 78
ON SELECTION PAD 78
ON SELECTION POPUP 78
PACK 78
PARAMETERS 79
PLAY MACRO 79
PRINTJOB/ENDPRINTJOB 80
PRIVATE/PUBLIC 81
PROCEDURE 82
PROTECT 83
PUBLIC 84
QUIT 84
READ 85
RECALL 85
REINDEX 86
RELEASE 86
RENAME 87
REPLACE 88

REPLACE FROM ARRAY 89
REPORT FORM 90
RESET 91
RESTORE 92
RESUME 93
RETRY 93
RETURN 94
ROLLBACK 95
RUN/! 95
SAVE 96
SCAN/ENDSCAN 97
SEEK 98
SELECT 99
SET 100
SHOW MENU 105
SHOW POPUP 105
SKIP 105
SORT 106
STORE 107
SUM 107
SUSPEND 108
TEXT, ENDTEXT 108
TOTAL 109
TYPE 110
UNLOCK 111
UPDATE 111
USE 112
WAIT 113
ZAP 114

dBASE IV FUNCTIONS 115

LOW-LEVEL FILE I/O FUNCTIONS 127

SYSTEM MEMORY VARIABLES 129

SQL COMMAND REFERENCE 133

SQL FUNCTIONS 137

INDEX 139

INTRODUCTION

dBASE IV 2.0 Quick Reference covers all dBASE IV commands, dBASE IV functions, and SQL commands to help you use this powerful package effectively. In this book, each dBASE IV command is presented in the same format: the purpose appears first, followed by the proper syntax, step-by-step procedures, and a Notes section that contains additional comments and hints.

In the statement of syntax, the command appears uppercase and in blue, such as COMMAND. Keys you press and text you type also appear in blue. Variable information appears in lowercase italic enclosed in angle brackets, such as *<information>*. Do not type the brackets when you enter the information. Optional command options appear in uppercase, enclosed in square brackets, such as [COMMAND]. Do not type the brackets when you enter the command.

This book also includes instructions for performing equivalent operations from the dBASE IV Control Center. These instructions are not listed when an equivalent operation is not available directly from the Control Center.

COMMAND REFERENCE

=

See *STORE*.

?/??

Purpose

Displays information on-screen if **SET CONSOLE** is **ON**. Sends output to the printer if **SET PRINTER** is **ON**, or to a file if SET ALTERNATE is **ON** and an alternate file is specified with SET ALTERNATE TO.

Command Syntax

?/?? [<*expression-1*> [PICTURE <*expC*>] [FUNCTION <*function-list*>] [AT <*expN*>] [STYLE <*font-number*>]] [,<*expression-2*>...] [,]

From the dot prompt

To display the result of an expression or value on the next line, issue the ? command. The ?? command displays the information without advancing to the next line.

Enclose STYLE options in double quotes. Following are the style font options:

B	Bold
I	Italic
U	Underline
R	Superscript (raised)
L	Subscript (lowered)

You also can use the numbers 1 through 5 to designate user-defined fonts with STYLE.

You can control the formatting of output with FUNCTION options (see *@...SAY/GET*). Following are additional FUNCTION options you can use with **?/??**:

Function	Description
H <*n*>	Word-wraps memo fields.
V <*n*>	Stretches a field vertically with column width of *n* characters.
;	Wraps text at semicolon.

???

Purpose

Sends output, such as printer control codes, directly to the printer.

Command Syntax

??? *<expC>*

From the dot prompt

Sends printer commands without moving the print head with the **???** commands. You can use control character identifiers or ASCII codes, surrounded by curly braces, literal strings, or the **CHR**( ) function. The following commands, for example, are equivalent and send an Escape-X to the printer:

```
??? "{ESC}X"
???  CHR(27) + "X"
??? "{27}{88}"
??? "{27}X"
```

!

See *RUN/!*.

*/&&

See *NOTE*.

@...SAY/GET

Purpose

Positions the cursor and displays or accepts information in a specified format.

Command Syntax

@ *<row>*,*<col>* [SAY *<expression>* [PICTURE *<expC>*] [FUNCTION *<function-list>*]] [GET *<variable>* [[OPEN] WINDOW *<window-name>*] [PICTURE*<expC>*] [FUNCTION *<function-list>*] [RANGE [REQUIRED] [*<low>*,] [,] [,*<high>*]] [VALID [REQUIRED] *<condition>* [ERROR *<expC>*]] [WHEN *<condition>*] [DEFAULT *<expression>*] [MESSAGE *<expC*]] [COLOR [*<standard>*] [,*<enhanced>*]]

From the dot prompt

1. To position and display screen and printer information, use the @...SAY command. A SET DEVICE TO PRINTER command causes all following **@...SAY** commands to be sent to the printer. A SET DEVICE TO FILE command directs output to a disk file. SET DEVICE TO SCREEN redirects **@...SAY** commands back to the screen.
2. To specify an input area for user input, use the @...GET command. To restrict the size and type of input, use the PICTURE clause.
3. To suggest a preset value for an **@...GET**, use the DEFAULT option.
4. The **VALID** clause specifies the condition the input must meet, otherwise the `Editing condition not satisfied` error message appears. To specify a custom error message, use the ERROR option.

You can use the following format functions using the PICTURE or FUNCTION option:

!	Allows any character to convert to uppercase
^	Displays in scientific notation

$	Displays in currency format
(	Encloses negative numbers in parentheses
A	Specifies alphabetic characters only
B	Left-aligns numbers in **@...SAY**
C	Displays **CR** (credit) after a positive number
D	Uses **SET DATE** format
E	Uses European date format
I	Centers text in **@...SAY**
J	Right-aligns text in **@...SAY**
L	Displays numeric fields that contain leading zeros
M	Multiple-choice list for **GET**
R	Displays but does not store literal characters
S<*n*>	Scrolls horizontally within field width of <*n*>
T	Trims leading and trailing blanks
X	Displays **DB** (debit) after negative numbers
Z	Displays zeros as blanks

From the Control Center

To create a screen form, choose <create> from the Forms column.

Notes

Row coordinates on a standard monitor screen range from 0 to 23, and column coordinates range from 0 to 79.

To activate any **@...GET** command issued since the last **CLEAR/CLEAR ALL/CLEAR GETS** or **READ** command was executed, use the READ command.

@...TO/FILL/CLEAR/SCROLL

Purpose

Draws boxes or changes the color of specified areas of the screen.

Command Syntax

@<*row-1*>,<*col-1*> TO <*row-2*>,<*col-2*> [DOUBLE/PANEL/<*border-definition-string*>] [COLOR <*color-attribute*>]

@<*row-1*>,<*col-1*> FILL TO <*row-2*>,<*col-2*> [COLOR <*color-attribute*>]

From the dot prompt

The following commands draw and fill a box on-screen:

@ 08,15 to 14,60 double color r/w

@ 09,16 fill to 13,59 color w/n

From the Control Center

1. Choose the <create> option from the Forms column of the Control Center.
2. To draw a double-line box, choose the Layout/Box/Double options.
3. To anchor the upper-left corner of the box, position the cursor at the desired location and press Enter. To stretch the box, use the arrow keys and press Enter to complete the task.

4. To select the box, press F6.
5. Choose Display from the Words menu. Choose the foreground and background colors you want. To select the color combination and exit the menus, press Ctrl-End.

@...CLEAR/SCROLL

Purpose

Clears a specified portion of the screen, or moves a section of the screen contents to a new screen location.

Command Syntax

@<*row-1*>,<*col-1*> CLEAR [TO <*row-2*>,<*col-2*>]

@ <*row-1*>,<*col-1*> TO <*row-2*>,<*col-2*> SCROLL [UP/DOWN/LEFT/RIGHT] [BY <*expN*>] [WRAP]

From the dot prompt

The following command clears a section of the screen:

```
@ 08,15 clear to 10,60
```

The following command shifts the specified section of the screen up 2 rows:

```
@ 12,10 TO 14,20 SCROLL UP BY 2
```

ACCEPT

Purpose

Prompts a user for a keyboard entry and stores the entry to a memory variable.

Command Syntax

ACCEPT [<*prompt*>] TO <*memvar*>

From the dot prompt

Issue the ACCEPT command from the dot prompt or in a program.

Note

You also can use the INPUT and WAIT commands to accept user input; however, the @...GET command offers more flexibility by its use of optional formats and templates.

ACTIVATE MENU

See *DEFINE MENU/DEFINE PAD.*

ACTIVATE POPUP

See *DEFINE POPUP.*

ACTIVATE SCREEN

Purpose

Enables the entire screen, rather than a predefined window, to be used or active. Other windows may be scrolled or cleared from the screen.

Command Syntax

ACTIVATE SCREEN

From the dot prompt

Use the ACTIVATE SCREEN command in a program to send output to the full screen rather than the active window.

ACTIVATE WINDOW

See *DEFINE WINDOW.*

APPEND

Purpose

Adds records to the end of a dBASE IV datafile.

Command Syntax

APPEND [BLANK]/[NOORGANIZE]

From the dot prompt

1. To open the datafile, issue the USE command.
2. Type APPEND and press Enter. A blank record appears on-screen. This is called the Append mode.
3. Type the data in each field of the blank record. When the record is filled, another blank record becomes available.
4. Press Ctrl-End to exit Append mode.

APPEND BLANK adds a blank record to the datafile but does not place the user in Append mode. The NORGANIZE option suppresses the Organize menu when in Append mode.

From the Control Center

1. Position the highlight on a file and press Enter to select it.
2. When prompted, choose the Display Data option.
3. Choose Add New Records from the Records menu.

Note

To move to the preceding and next record in Append mode, press PgUp and PgDn. To end the append activity, press Ctrl-End.

APPEND FROM

Purpose

Adds records to a database from an array or another database.

Command Syntax

APPEND FROM ARRAY *<array-name>* [REINDEX] [FOR *<condition>*]

APPEND FROM *<file-name>*/? [[TYPE] *<file-type>*] [REINDEX] [FOR *<condition>*]

From the dot prompt

1. Before you use the **APPEND FROM ARRAY** command, make sure that the array is declared and filled with information.
2. To append records from another file, issue the APPEND FROM command.

From the Control Center

1. Position the highlight on a file and press Enter to select it.
2. When prompted, choose the Modify Structure/ Order option.
3. Use the arrow keys to open the Append menu and choose an option.
4. Choose either Append Records from dBASE File or Copy Records from non-dBASE File.

Notes

The array elements of information must be in the same order as the record structure. The first array element value is moved to the first field in the record, and so on. dBASE IV ignores extra array elements (length only). A record for each row of the array is added to the datafile automatically.

Valid <*file-types*> are dBASEII, DELIMITED, DELIMITED WITH BLANK, DELIMITED WITH <*character*>, DIF (VisiCalc), FW2, FW3, and FW4 (Framework II, III and IV), RPD (RapidFile), SDF (System Data Format ASCII file), SYLK (MultiPlan), and WKS (Lotus 1-2-3).

Blank rows in any spreadsheet file type are converted to blank records for the datafile.

APPEND MEMO

Purpose

Reads a file into the specified memo field of the current record.

Command Syntax

APPEND MEMO <*memo-field-name*> FROM <*file-name*> [OVERWRITE]

From the dot prompt

To replace the existing memo field data, include the OVERWRITE clause; otherwise, the new information is appended to the existing memo data.

From the Control Center

1. Position the highlight on a datafile name and press Enter to select it.
2. When prompted, choose the Display Data option.
3. Display the record you want to edit, or choose Add New Records from the Records menu.
4. Position the cursor in the memo field marker, and then press Ctrl-Home to open the memo field.
5. Press F10 to access the menus, and then choose Words, Write/Read Text File, or Read Text from File, and specify the file name when prompted.

Note

The database must include a memo field before you issue this command. An error occurs if you specify a field that does not exist or is not a memo field.

ASSIST

Purpose

Accesses the dBASE IV Control Center screen rather than the dot prompt.

Command Syntax

ASSIST

From the dot prompt

1. Type ASSIST or press F2.
2. To return to the dot prompt from the Control Center screen, choose Exit to Dot Prompt from the Exit menu.

Note

To begin every session at the Control Center, include the statement COMMAND=ASSIST in your CONFIG.DB file.

AVERAGE

See *CALCULATE*.

BEGIN/END TRANSACTION

Purpose

Marks the start and end of a transaction, during which dBASE IV logs changes made to records and new files that are created. The **ROLLBACK** command can restore database files to the state in which they were before you began the transaction.

Command Syntax

BEGIN TRANSACTION [<*path-name*>]
<*commands*>

END TRANSACTION

ROLLBACK [<*datafile-name*>]

From the dot prompt

To start transaction logging, issue the BEGIN TRANSACTION and follow any transaction commands with the END TRANSACTION command. To restore the database file to its pre-transaction state, use the ROLLBACK command.

Notes

Each **BEGIN TRANSACTION** command line must have a matching **END TRANSACTION** command line.

Do not include the **CLEAR ALL**, **CLOSE**, **CONVERT**, **CREATE VIEW**, **DELETE FILE**, **ERASE**, **INSERT**, **MODIFY STRUCTURE**, **PACK**, **RENAME**, or **ZAP** commands in transaction processing. Also, avoid using any command that closes open files or overwrites existing files.

BLANK

Purpose

Fills records or fields with blanks.

Command Syntax

BLANK [FIELDS <*field-list*>/LIKE/EXCEPT <*skeleton*>] [REINDEX] [<*scope*>] [FOR <condition>] [WHILE <condition>]

From the dot prompt

1. Issue the BLANK command from the dot prompt or from within a program.
2. Optionally specify a condition to select records to be blanked, or select fields to be blanked. You can use the **REINDEX** option to rebuild indexes after records are blanked.

From the Control Center

To blank the current record, choose Blank record from the Records menu while in the Edit or Browse screens. In the Browse screen, choose Blank Field from the Fields menu.

Note

You cannot blank fields designated as read-only.

BROWSE

Purpose

Displays records of a datafile in a tabular format, and enables records to be modified.

Reminder

You can use the following keys while using the Browse Mode:

Key(s)	Function
Ctrl-U	Marks or unmarks a record for deletion.
Ctrl-Q or **Esc**	Ends the Browse session without saving changes to current record.
Ctrl-W or **Ctrl-End**	Ends the Edit session and saves any changes to current record.
PgUp	Moves to the previous screen.
PgDn	Moves to the next screen.
↑	Moves to the previous record.
↓	Moves to the next record.
→	Moves to the next character.
←	Moves to the previous character.
Tab	Moves to the next field.
Shift-Tab	Moves to the previous field.

Command Syntax

BROWSE [NOINIT] [NOFOLLOW] [NOAPPEND] [NOMENU] [NOEDIT] [NODELETE] [NOCLEAR] [NOORGANIZE]

[COMPRESS] [FORMAT] [LOCK *<expN>*] [WIDTH *<expN>*] [FREEZE *<field-name>*] [WINDOW *<window-name>*] [FIELDS *<field-name-1>* [/R] [/*<column-width>*] /*<calculated-field-name-1>=<expression-1>* [,*<field-name-2>* [/R] [/*<column-width>*] /*<calculated-field-2> = <expression-2>*]...]

From the dot prompt

1. Open the datafile with the USE command.
2. Type BROWSE and any desired options, and press Enter.
3. View and change any information in the database, and then press Ctrl-End to save the changes and return to the dot prompt.
4. To close the open database, type USE and press Enter.

From the Control Center

1. Position the highlight on the datafile name.
2. To access the Browse mode, press F2. To alternate between Browse and Edit modes, press F2.
3. Choose the Exit option from the Exit menu.

Notes

Use the Go To menu to move to the top or bottom record, to move to a particular record number, or to search for a specified value in a selected field.

To prevent the user from adding new records, include the NOAPPEND clause, or use NOEDIT to prevent editing of the records. To exit without saving changes to the current record, press Esc or Ctrl-Q.

CALCULATE/AVERAGE/SUM

Purpose

CALCULATE performs financial and statistical calculations, **AVERAGE** and **SUM** compute averages and totals, and **COUNT** determines the number of records matching the specified condition.

Command Syntax

CALCULATE [<*scope*>]<*option-list*> [FOR <*condition*>] [WHILE <*condition*>] [TO <*memvar-list*>/TO ARRAY <*array-name*>]

AVERAGE [<*expN-list*>] [<*scope*>] [FOR<*condition*>] [WHILE<*condition*>] [TO <*memvar-list*>/TO ARRAY <*array-name*>]

COUNT [TO <*memvar*>] [<*scope*>] [FOR <*condition*>] [WHILE <condition>]

SUM [<*expN-list*>] [TO <*memvar-list*>/TO ARRAY <*array-name*>] [<*scope*>] [FOR <*condition*>] [WHILE <*condition*>]

From the dot prompt

1. Open the datafile with the USE command.
2. Issue the command, and optionally specify a memory variable to store the result of the calculation.

From the Control Center

1. Select a datafile in the Data column, press Enter, and then choose Use File.
2. Choose the <create> option in the Queries column and press Enter.

3. In the query design screen, position the cursor under a numeric field in the file skeleton.
4. To display the expression-builder box, press Shift-F1. Select from the QBE Operator column the operation you want to perform (Average, Count, Sum, and so on) and press Enter.
5. To display the results, press F2. To return to the Control Center, press Esc or choose Exit from the Exit menu.

Notes

The *<option-list>* for **CALCULATE** can include the following functions:

AVG(*<expN>*)

CNT( )

MAX(*<exp>*)

MIN(*<exp>*)

NPV(*<rate>*,*<flows>*,*<initial>*)

STD(*<expN>*)

SUM(*<expN>*)

VAR(*<expN>*)

When issuing the calculation commands at the dot prompt, be sure **SET TALK** is **ON** if you want the results to appear on-screen; or, to display the values stored in a memory variable, use the ? or @...SAYcommands.

CALL

Purpose

Calls from memory a binary program module.

Command Syntax

CALL *<module-name>* [WITH *<expression-list>*]

From the dot prompt

1. To read the binary program from the disk, use the LOAD command.
2. To run the binary program, use the CALL command line.
3. To remove the binary program from memory, issue the RELEASE MODULE command.

Note

Before the binary program can be run with the CALL command, you must load it with the LOAD command.

CANCEL

Purpose

Stops program execution, closes open program files, and returns you to the dot prompt.

Command Syntax

CANCEL

From the dot prompt

To cancel the program and return control to the dot prompt, include in the program the CANCEL command.

From the Control Center

To stop the processing of a query, report, or program, press Esc. When prompted to `Cancel`, `Suspend`, or `Ignore`, choose `Cancel` to return to the Control Center.

Note

CANCEL does not close the open database or procedure files. To close those files, use the CLOSE DATABASE or CLOSE PROCEDURE commands. To temporarily halt execution of a program file, use SUSPEND.

CHANGE

See *EDIT*.

CLEAR

Purpose

Erases the screen or a window. You also can use this command to close datafiles, release memory variables, field lists, windows, pop-ups, or menus, and to clear the type-ahead buffer.

Command Syntax

CLEAR [ALL/FIELDS/GETS/MEMORY/MENUS
/POPUPS/SCREEN/TYPEAHEAD/WINDOWS]

From the dot prompt

1. To close open datafiles and the active catalog, and to release all memory variables, arrays, pop-ups, and menu definitions, include the ALL clause.
2. To remove information selectively, use the appropriate clause.

Note

Using the CLEAR command without any of the options only clears the screen.

CLOSE

Purpose

Closes an open datafile. Also closes Alternate, Format, Index, Printer and Procedure files.

Command Syntax

CLOSE ALL/ALTERNATE/DATABASES
/FORMAT/INDEXES/PROCEDURE/PRINTER

From the dot prompt

To close all open database files, issue the CLOSE DATABASES command, or specify the type of file you want to close (**ALTERNATE**, **FORMAT**, **INDEX**, **PROCEDURE**). CLOSE PRINTER closes a file opened with the **SET PRINTER TO FILE** command.

From the Control Center

1. Position the highlight on the name of the open datafile name in the Data column, and press Enter.
2. Choose Close File.

COMPILE

Purpose

Creates an executable object code file from a dBASE IV source code file.

Command Syntax

COMPILE <*file-name*> [RUNTIME]

From the dot prompt

Save the new or changed program source code file on disk. To compile the source code file into an object code file, use the COMPILE command.

From the Control Center

Select the program file in the Applications column and press Enter. Choose Run Application. If the program is not yet compiled, dBASE IV compiles the program automatically before running it.

Notes

Before dBASE IV runs a program, it checks the date and time stamp of the .PRG (source) file against the .DBO (object) file. If the source code has changed since it was last compiled, you must recompile it to utilize the most recent changes. Normally, dBASE IV recompiles the code automatically. To turn on or off automatic program recompilation, use the SET DEVELOPMENT command.

Command lines in the program file are checked for proper syntax during the compilation process. If an error is encountered, a message and the line number on which the error occurred appear.

CONTINUE

See *LOCATE*.

CONVERT

Purpose

Changes the structure of a single-user datafile by adding a new field for multiuser access.

Command Syntax

CONVERT [TO <*expN*>]

From the dot prompt

1. Open the database file with the USE command.
2. To insert a character field called _dbaselock in the datafile structure, issue the CONVERT command.

Notes

The optional numeric expression specifies the length of the added _dbaselock field. The length can range from 8 to 24 characters, with a 16-character default size. The _dbaselock field stores the following values:

Count	A 2-byte hexadecimal number used to record the number of times the record changes.
Time	A 3-byte hexadecimal number that records the time a lock occurs.
Date	A 3-byte hexadecimal number that records the date a lock occurs.
Name	The log-in name of the user that locked the record.

COPY

Purpose

Makes a copy of all records or selected records from the active database file to a new file or an array. You can use different forms of the **COPY** command to copy entire files, indexes, memo field data, or a datafile structure.

Command Syntax

COPY TO *<file-name>* [[TYPE] *<file-type>*]/ [[WITH] PRODUCTION] [FIELDS *<field-list>*] [*<scope>*] [FOR *<condition>*] [WHILE *<condition>*]

COPY STRUCTURE TO *<file-name>* [FIELDS *<field-list>*] [[WITH] PRODUCTION]

COPY TO *<file-name>* STRUCTURE EXTENDED

COPY TO ARRAY *<array-name>* [FIELDS *<field-list>*] [*<scope>*] [FOR *<condition>*] [WHILE *<condition>*]

COPY FILE *<file-name>* TO *<file-name>*

COPY INDEXES *<index-file-list>* [TO *<multiple-index-file>*]

COPY MEMO *<memo-field-name>* TO *<file-name>* [ADDITIVE]

COPY TAG *<tag-name>* [OF *<multiple-index-file>*] TO *<index-file-name>*

From the dot prompt

1. Open a database file with the USE command.
2. To copy contents, structure, or indexes of the database file to a new file, or to copy records to an array, issue the appropriate COPY command.
3. Close the open database file with the USE or CLOSE command.

Notes

Before copying records to an array with COPY TO ARRAY, you must use the DECLARE command to establish the array. You use the REPLACE FROM ARRAY command to restore values to a database from an array.

COUNT

See *CALCULATE*.

CREATE APPLICATION

Purpose

Invokes the dBASE IV Applications Generator, used to design menus and other objects and to generate dBASE program code.

Command Syntax

CREATE/MODIFY APPLICATION *<file-name>*/?

From the dot prompt

To access the Applications Generator. Provide a file name for the application, issue CREATE APPLICATION from the dot prompt, or use a ? for a list of application files in the current catalog.

From the Control Center

Choose the <create> option from the Applications column. When prompted, choose Applications Generator.

CREATE FROM

Purpose

Creates a new dBASE IV database file from a structure created with the COPY STRUCTURE EXTENDED command.

Command Syntax

CREATE *<file-name>* FROM *<structure-extended-file>*

From the dot prompt

1. Open a database file with the USE command.
2. To create a structure file based on the currently active database file, use the COPY STRUCTURE EXTENDED command.
3. Issue the CREATE FROM command, specifying the name of the new database file you want to create and the name of the structure file.

CREATE/MODIFY LABEL

Purpose

Invokes the dBASE IV label design screen that enables you to design and print labels.

Command Syntax

CREATE/MODIFY LABEL *<file-name>*/?

From the dot prompt

1. Open a database file with the USE command.
2. Issue the CREATE LABEL command, specifying the file name for the label design file. To choose from a list of label files in the current catalog, use the MODIFY LABEL ? command.

From the Control Center

1. Select a database file in the Data column, press Enter, and then choose Use File.
2. Choose the <create> option in the Labels column and press Enter.

Notes

To print labels from the Control Center, choose a file from the Label column, press Enter, and then choose Print Labels.

To print labels from the label design screen, choose Begin Printing from the Print menu.

To print labels from the dot prompt, use the LABEL FORM command.

CREATE/MODIFY QUERY/VIEW

Purpose

Invokes the query design screen that enables you to perform sorting and calculations on database records, and specify selection criteria to be used in extracting records from database files.

Command Syntax

CREATE/MODIFY QUERY *<file-name>*/?
CREATE/MODIFY VIEW *<file-name>*/?

From the dot prompt

To choose from a list of existing query files, issue the CREATE QUERY command, specifying the file name for the query file, or include the ? clause.

From the Control Center

1. Select a database file in the Data column, press Enter, and then choose Use File.
2. Choose the <create> option in the Queries column, and press Enter.

Notes

To activate a query file from the dot prompt, or from within a program, use the SET VIEW TO command.

To activate a query from the Control Center, select the query file from the Queries column and press Enter.

CREATE/MODIFY REPORT

Purpose

Invokes the dBASE IV report design screen that enables you to design and print reports.

Command Syntax

CREATE/MODIFY REPORT *<file-name>* /?

From the dot prompt

1. Open a database file with the USE command.
2. Issue the CREATE REPORT command, specifying the file name for the report design file. To choose from a list of report files in the current catalog, use the MODIFY REPORT ? command.

From the Control Center

1. Select a database file in the Data column, press Enter, and then choose Use File.
2. Choose the <create> option in the Reports column and press Enter.

Notes

To print reports from the Control Center, select a file from the Reports column, press Enter, and then choose Print Reports.

To print reports from the report design screen, choose Begin Printing from the Print menu.

To print reports from the dot prompt, use the REPORT FORM command.

CREATE/MODIFY SCREEN

Purpose

Invokes the dBASE IV forms design screen. This enables you to design data-entry screens and format the way in which data appears.

Command Syntax

CREATE/MODIFY SCREEN *<file-name>*/?

From the dot prompt

1. Open a database file with the USE command.
2. Issue the CREATE SCREEN command, specifying the file name for the screen form design file. To choose from a list of screen form files in the current catalog, use the MODIFY SCREEN ? command.

From the Control Center

1. Select a database file in the Data column, press Enter, and then choose Use File.
2. Choose the <create> option in the Forms column and press Enter.

Notes

To activate a screen form from the Control Center, choose the screen form file from the Forms column, press Enter, and then choose Display Data.

To activate a screen form from the dot prompt, or from within a program, use the SET FORMAT TO command.

CREATE or MODIFY STRUCTURE

Purpose

Invokes the dBASE IV database design screen, which enables you to create or change a dBASE IV database file structure.

Command Syntax

CREATE *<file-name>*

MODIFY STRUCTURE

From the dot prompt

1. To create a new datafile, type CREATE and a file name. The database design screen appears.

2. Enter the name, data type, and length for each field you want to include in the datafile, and specify index tags to be created. Press Ctrl-End to save the design and return to the dot prompt.
3. To change the datafile structure at any time, open the datafile with the USE command, and then issue the MODIFY STRUCTURE command.

From the Control Center

1. Choose the <create> option in the Data column. The database design screen appears.
2. Enter the name, data type, and length for each field you want to include in the datafile, and specify index tags to be created. Press Ctrl-End to save the design and return to the Control Center.
3. When prompted, type a file name for the new file and press Enter.
4. When prompted to input data now, press N or Y.
5. To change a database structure, select the file in the Data column of the Control Center and press Shift-F2 to invoke the database design screen.

CAUTION: When modifying a database structure, do not change field names at the same time you insert or delete fields. Also, do not change a field name at the same time you change the width or type because data may be lost.

DEACTIVATE MENU

See *DEFINE MENU/DEFINE PAD*.

DEACTIVATE POPUP

See *DEFINE POPUP*.

DEACTIVATE WINDOW

See *DEFINE WINDOW*.

DEBUG

Purpose

Runs the dBASE IV debugger that enables you to test programs and procedures.

Command Syntax

DEBUG *<file-name>*/*<procedure-name>* [WITH *<parameter-list>*]

From the dot prompt

1. Issue the DEBUG command, specifying the program or procedure and any parameters.
2. In the debugger screen, type the key representing the action you want to perform. To access the Help panel, which displays a list of available actions, press F1.

3. To Quit the debugger and return to the dot prompt, press Q.

Notes

To exit to the dot prompt temporarily, type U (Suspend) in the debugger screen. To return to the debugger screen, use RESUME, or to end the debugger session and remain at the dot prompt, use CANCEL.

DECLARE

Purpose

Establishes an array of memory variables.

Command Syntax

DECLARE <*array-name-1*> [{<*number-of-rows*>,} <*number-of-columns*>] {,<*array-name-2*> [{<*number-of-rows*>,} <*number-of-columns*>]...}

From the dot prompt

1. To create an array, issue the DECLARE command from the dot prompt or in a program.
2. Assign values to the elements with the = or STORE command.

Note

An array can have one or two dimensions, with a single dimension being limited to 65,535 elements or by the amount of memory available.

DEFINE BAR

See *DEFINE POPUP*.

DEFINE BOX

Purpose

Defines boxes to be printed around text in reports.

Command Syntax

DEFINE BOX FROM <*print-column*> TO <*print-column*> HEIGHT <*expN*> [AT LINE <*print-line*>] [SINGLE/DOUBLE/<*border-definition-string*>]

From the dot prompt

1. Issue the DEFINE BOX command from the dot prompt or in a program.
2. To enable box printing, set the _box memory variable to true (`.T.`). When the print line (`_plineno`) equals the top row of the box, the box will print as part of the output.

From the Control Center

When creating a report format, choose the Box option from the Layout menu.

DEFINE MENU/DEFINE PAD

Purpose

DEFINE MENU assigns a name to a bar menu and optionally specifies a message to appear with the menu. **DEFINE PAD** is used to define each pad of a bar menu.

ACTIVATE MENU is used to display the menu, and **DEACTIVATE MENU** removes the menu from the screen. **SHOW MENU** displays the menu without activating it. **ON SELECTION PAD** executes a command when a pad is selected.

Command Syntax

DEFINE MENU *<menu-name>* [MESSAGE *<expC>*]

DEFINE PAD *<pad-name>* OF *<menu-name>*
PROMPT *<expC>* [AT *<row>*,*<col>*] [MESSAGE*<expC>*]

ACTIVATE MENU *<menu-name>* [PAD *<pad-name>*]
DEACTIVATE MENU

ON SELECTION PAD *<pad-name>* OF *<menu-name>* [*<command>*]
SHOW MENU *<menu-name>* [PAD *<pad-name>*]

From the dot prompt

1. To define the menu, use DEFINE MENU, and to define the pads of the menu, use DEFINE PAD.
2. To specify actions for each **DEFINE PAD** command, issue an ON SELECTION PAD command.
3. Activate the menu with the ACTIVATE MENU command. When finished with a menu, use the DEACTIVATE MENU command.

From the Control Center

Choose the <create> option in the Application column to create a new program using the Applications Generator. To specify the type of menu you want to create, use the Design menu in the Applications Generator.

Note

To remove menu definition from memory, use the RELEASE MENUS command.

DEFINE POPUP

Purpose

DEFINE POPUP defines a pop-up menu window name, location, border, prompts and message line. **DEFINE BAR** defines a single option in the pop-up menu. **ON SELECTION POPUP** specifies a command to execute when a bar is selected.

ACTIVATE POPUP makes the pop-up menu the active menu. **DEACTIVATE POPUP** removes the pop-up menu from the screen. **SHOW POPUP** displays the menu without activating it.

Command Syntax

DEFINE POPUP *<popup-name>* FROM *<row-1>*,*<col-1>* [TO *<row-2>*,*<col-2>*] [PROMPT FIELD *<field-name>*/PROMPT FILES [LIKE *<skeleton>*]/PROMPT STRUCTURE] [MESSAGE *<expC>*]

ACTIVATE POPUP *<popup-name>*

DEACTIVATE POPUP

DEFINE BAR *<line-number>* OF *<popup-name>*

PROMPT *<expC>* [MESSAGE *<expC>*] [SKIP [FOR *<condition>*]]

ON SELECTION POPUP *<popup-name>*/ALL [BLANK] [*<command>*]

SHOW POPUP *<popup-name>*

From the dot prompt

1. To define the menu, use DEFINE POPUP. To define each bar in the menu, use DEFINE BAR.
2. To specify actions for each **DEFINE BAR** command, issue an ON SELECTION POPUP command.
3. Activate the menu with the ACTIVATE POPUP command. When finished with a pop-up menu, use the DEACTIVATE POPUP command.

From the Control Center

To create a new program using the Applications Generator, choose the <create> option in the Application column. To define menus, use the Design menu in the Applications Generator.

Note

To remove a pop-up definition from memory, use the RELEASE POPUP command.

DEFINE WINDOW

Purpose

DEFINE WINDOW defines the size and location of a window, as well as the border and colors.

ACTIVATE WINDOW displays the window and makes it the active window. **DEACTIVATE WINDOW** removes the window from the screen.

MOVE WINDOW relocates the window on-screen. The **BY** option enables you to specify a number of rows or columns to move relative to the current location.

Command Syntax

DEFINE WINDOW *<window-name>* FROM *<row-1>,<col-1>* TO *<row-2>,<col-2>* [DOUBLE /PANEL/NONE/*<border-definition-string>*] [COLOR [*<standard>*] [,*<enhanced>*] [,*<frame>*]]

ACTIVATE WINDOW *<window-name-list>* /ALL

DEACTIVATE WINDOW *<window-name-list>* /ALL

MOVE WINDOW *<window-name>* TO *<row>,<column>*/BY *<delta-row>,<delta-column>*

From the dot prompt

1. To define the window, specifying the window name, screen coordinates, type of border and colors, use the DEFINE WINDOW command.
2. To display the window, issue the ACTIVATE WINDOW command.
3. To reposition the window if needed, use the MOVE WINDOW command.
4. To remove the window from the screen, issue a DEACTIVATE WINDOW command.

Note

To remove window definitions from memory, use the RELEASE WINDOW command.

DELETE/PACK

Purpose

DELETE marks records to be deleted from the active database file. **PACK** removes the marked records from the database file.

Command Syntax

DELETE [<*scope*>] [FOR <*condition*>] [WHILE <*condition*>]

PACK

From the dot prompt

1. Open a database file with the USE command.
2. To delete a single record, use SEEK, GOTO, or LOCATE to find the record you want to delete.
3. Type DELETE and press Enter.
4. To delete all records meeting a condition, issue the DELETE command with the appropriate options.
5. Issue the PACK command to remove records marked for deletion from the active database file.

From the Control Center

1. To view records, choose a file in the Data column, and then press F2.
2. From the Browse or Edit screens, to locate a record you want to delete, use the arrow keys or the Go To menu.

3. Highlight the record you want to delete, and then press Ctrl-U, or choose Mark Record for Deletion from the Records menu.
4. To remove the deletion mark, press Ctrl-U again, or choose Clear Deletion Mark from the Records menu.
5. To return to the Control Center, choose Exit from the Exit menu.

Notes

To remove the deletion mark from records from the dot prompt, use the RECALL command.

Remember that **DELETE** only marks the records for deletion. Records are not actually removed until you issue the PACK command.

To specify if records marked for deletion are used in dBASE operations, use the SET DELETED command.

DELETE FILE

See *ERASE*.

DELETE TAG

Purpose

Removes an index tag from a multiple index (.MDX) file.

Command Syntax

DELETE TAG <*tag-name*-1> [OF <*multiple-index-file-name*>] [,<*tag-name-2*> [OF <*multiple-index-file-name*>] ...]

From the dot prompt

To remove an existing index tag from a multiple index file, issue a DELETE TAG command. If no file name is specified, the currently active .MDX file is assumed.

From the Control Center

1. Select a file in the Data column, and press Shift-F2.
2. From the database design screen, choose the Remove Unwanted Index Tag option from the Organize menu. Select the index tags you want to remove from the multiple index file.
3. Choose Save Changes and Exit from the Exit menu, or press Ctrl-End to return to the Control Center.

DEXPORT

Purpose

Creates a Binary Named List (BNL) file from a screen, report, or label design file.

Command Syntax

DEXPORT SCREEN/REPORT/LABEL
<*file-name*> [TO <*BNL-file-name*>]

From the dot prompt

Issue the DEXPORT command from the dot prompt or from within a program and specify the type of file you want to create.

Note

dBASE IV uses the following file extensions for BNL files:

File	Extension
Screens	.SNL
Reports	.FNL
Labels	.LNL

DIR

Purpose

Displays a directory of database files.

Command Syntax

DIRECTORY/DIR [[ON] <*drive*>:] [[LIKE] [<*path*>] <*skeleton*>]

From the dot prompt

Use the DIR command to list database (.DBF) files in the current disk, or use the *.* skeleton to display all files in the directory. You optionally can specify another drive or directory path.

From the Control Center

1. Choose the DOS Utilities option from the Tools menu. The DOS Utilities window displays a directory of files in the current directory.

2. Use the Files menu to change the drive or subdirectory, or to specify the type of files you want to display.
3. Choose Exit to Control Center from the Exit menu.

Note

A DIR command without a path or skeleton lists only the .DBF files in the current directory.

DISPLAY

See *LIST*.

DO

Purpose

Runs dBASE IV programs.

Command Syntax

DO *<program-name>*/*<procedure-name>* [WITH *<parameter-list>*]

From the dot prompt

Run the program by issuing the DO command. If the program source code has changed since the last compilation, dBASE IV evaluates it for errors and recompiles it before running it.

From the Control Center

1. Position the highlight on the selected option in the Application column and press Enter.
2. When prompted, choose Run Application.

DO CASE/ENDCASE

Purpose

Controls program flow based on specified conditions.

Command Syntax

```
DO CASE
    [CASE <condition-1>
    <commands-1>]
    [CASE <condition-2>
    <commands>]
    ...
    [OTHERWISE
    <commands>]
ENDCASE
```

From the dot prompt

1. To mark the beginning and end of the command structure, use the DO CASE, ENDCASE command set.
2. Use a CASE command for each condition to be tested. If a **CASE** condition is evaluated as true (`.T.`), the commands following it are executed.

3. To specify commands to be executed if none of the **CASE** conditions are met, include the OTHERWISE command.

Note

Only the first **CASE** condition evaluated as true is acted upon. If no **CASE** conditions are met and no **OTHERWISE** statement exists, the next command after the **ENDCASE** statement is executed.

DO WHILE/ENDDO

Purpose

Executes a set of commands while a specified condition is met.

Command Syntax

```
DO WHILE <condition>
    <commands>
    [LOOP]
    [EXIT]
ENDDO
```

From the dot prompt

1. To mark the beginning and end of the **DO WHILE** loop and specify a condition that must be met for commands within the loop to be executed, use DO WHILE <*condition*> and ENDDO.

2. Include one or more commands to be executed repeatedly until the condition is no longer true.

3. Use the LOOP option to return execution to the start of the DO WHILE structure and prevent the execution of remaining commands in the structure. To pass control to the statement following the ENDDO command, use EXIT.

Notes

When using a **DO WHILE** loop to process records in a database file, include the SKIP command to move the record pointer to the next record after each record is processed. You also can use the SCAN command to process records in place of a **DO WHILE** loop.

EDIT/CHANGE

Purpose

Invokes the Edit screen, enabling you to view or change records in the active database file. The CHANGE command is the same as the EDIT command.

Command Syntax

EDIT [NOINIT] [NOFOLLOW] [NOAPPEND] [NOMENU] [NOEDIT] [NODELETE] [NOCLEAR] [NOORGANIZE] [<*record-number*>] [FIELDS <*field-list*>] [<*scope*>] [FOR <*condition*>] [WHILE <*condition*>]

CHANGE [NOINIT] [NOFOLLOW] [NOAPPEND] [NOMENU] [NOEDIT] [NODELETE] [NOCLEAR] [NOORGANIZE] [<*record-number*>] [FIELDS <*field-list*>] [<*scope*>] [FOR <*condition*>] [WHILE <*condition*>]

From the dot prompt

1. Open the database file with the USE command. To locate the record you want to change, use GOTO, LOCATE, SEEK, or FIND.
2. To display the Edit screen, type EDIT and press Enter.
3. Change the information you want.
4. To save the changes and return to the dot prompt, press Ctrl-End.

From the Control Center

1. Position the highlight on a file in the Data column.
2. To view the data, press F2. If the Use the Browse screen appears, press F2 again to access the Edit screen.

Notes

You can use the following keys while editing data:

Key(s)	Description
Ctrl-U	Flags or unflags a record for deletion.
Esc	Exits without saving changes to current record.
Ctrl-End	Ends the edit session and saves the data changes.
PgDn	Moves to the next screen.
PgUp	Moves to the previous screen.
Tab or ↓	Moves to the next field or record.

continues

Key(s)	Description
Shift-Tab or ↑	Moves to the previous field or record.
→	Moves to the next character.
←	Moves to the previous character.

To control the edit activity, include the NOINIT, NOFOLLOW, NOAPPEND, NOMENU, NOORGANIZE, NOEDIT, NODELETE, or NOCLEAR clauses.

To edit a particular record, specify the <*record-number*>. To specify the fields you want to appear on-screen, include the FIELDS <*field-list*> clause. To specify a range of datafile records, include the <*scope*>, FOR <*condition*>, and WHILE <*condition*> clauses.

To specify a screen format file to be used in the Edit mode, issue the SET FORMAT command before the EDIT command.

EJECT/EJECT PAGE

Purpose

EJECT advances paper in the printer to the top of the next page. **EJECT PAGE** advances output to the defined **ON PAGE** handler or the beginning of the next page.

Command Syntax

```
EJECT
EJECT PAGE
```

From the dot prompt

To instruct the printer to move the paper to the top of the next page, issue an EJECT command from the dot prompt or from within a program. To perform an operation, such as printing a header or footer, when printed output passes a particular line in the current page, use EJECT PAGE in a program.

From the Control Center

1. Select a file from the Reports or Labels column, and press Enter. When prompted, choose the Print Report or Print Labels option.
2. When the Print menu appears, choose the Eject Page Now option.

Note

To send output to the printer, use the SET DEVICE or SET PRINTER commands.

ERASE

Purpose

Deletes a file from the disk. **ERASE** and **DELETE FILE** are equivalent commands.

Command Syntax

ERASE *<file-name>*/?

DELETE FILE *<file-name>*/?

From the dot prompt

To remove the specified file from the disk, issue a DELETE FILE or ERASE command from the prompt or within a program. To display a list of files, use the ? option. You cannot erase an open file.

From the Control Center

1. Choose the DOS Utilities option from the Tools menu.
2. From the DOS Utilities window, press Enter to select and mark the file(s) you want to delete.
3. To erase the marked file(s), choose Delete from the Operations menu.
4. Choose Exit to Control Center from the Exit menu.

EXPORT

Purpose

Copies dBASE IV database records to a file in a format that can be used by other applications. You can export dBASE IV data to RapidFile, dBASE II, Lotus 1-2-3, PFS:File, or Framework versions II, III, and IV formats.

Command Syntax

EXPORT TO *<file-name>* [TYPE] RPD/ DBASEII/WK1/WKS/PFS/FW2/FW3/FW4 [FIELDS *<field-list>*] [*<scope>*] [FOR *<condition>*] [WHILE *<condition>*]

From the dot prompt

1. To open the dBASE IV datafile that contains the records you want to export, issue the USE command.
2. To specify the output file name, the type of file format you want, and any condition you will use to select records, use the EXPORT command.
3. When the exporting of records is complete, type USE at the dot prompt to close the datafile.

From the Control Center

1. Select the file you want in the Data column, and press Enter.
2. Choose the Export option from the Tools menu.
3. Select the export file format, and press Enter.
4. When prompted, type the name of the output file and press Enter.

Note

To copy records to dBASE IV format and various other formats, use the COPY TO command.

FIND

Purpose

Searches for data in an indexed field that matches the specified key. If a match is found, the record pointer moves to the record that contains the match.

Command Syntax

FIND <*literal-key*>

From the dot prompt

1. To open the database file, issue the USE command. If no production index file exists, specify an index file you want to use.
2. To search for a value in the key field, type FIND, and then type the value you are seeking.
3. To close the open datafile, type USE and press Enter.

From the Control Center

1. Select a file in the Data column, and press F2.
2. Highlight the field you want to search. Choose Index Key Search from the Go To menu.
3. Enter the value you are seeking. If the value is found, the highlight moves to the appropriate record.
4. To return to the Control Center, press Esc or choose the Exit option from the Exit menu.

Notes

To specify that the string for which you are searching must be the exact same length as the specified key, issue the SET EXACT ON command before you perform the search.

When using a search command in a program, you can use the FOUND( ) function to determine whether the desired record was found during the search.

To perform searches using expressions, use the SEEK command or the SEEK ( ) function.

FUNCTION

Purpose

Defines a user-defined function (UDF), which is a special type of procedure that returns a value you can use in a dBASE IV expression.

Command Syntax

FUNCTION *<user-defined-function-name>*
[PARAMETERS *<parameters>*]
[*<commands>*]
RETURN *<expression>*

From the dot prompt

In a program, start a user-defined function with the FUNCTION command and the name of the function you are defining. Include any optional parameters using the PARAMETERS statement, and the commands to be executed within the function. Use the RETURN statement to return the result of the function to the calling program.

Note

Do not use the name of an existing dBASE IV function as the name of your user-defined function.

GO/GOTO

Purpose

Moves the record pointer within the datafile.

Command Syntax

GO/GOTO BOTTOM/TOP [IN <*alias*>]
GO/GOTO [RECORD] <*record-number*> [IN <*alias*>] <*record-number*> [IN <*alias*>]

From the dot prompt

1. Open a datafile with the USE command.
2. Type GO followed by a space and the record number (such as GO 23), and press Enter.
3. To view the record, type EDIT and press Enter, or press F10. To return to the dot prompt, press Esc.
4. To move to the first or last record in the file, use the GO TOP or GO BOTTOM commands.

From the Control Center

1. Select a file in the Data column and press F2 to display the data.
2. Choose the Go To menu, and then choose Top Record, Last Record, or Record Number.
3. To return to the Control Center, choose Exit from the Exit menu.

HELP

Purpose

Displays the dBASE IV Help screen, which gives information about commands and functions.

Command Syntax

HELP [*<dBASE IV keyword>*]

From the dot prompt

1. Type HELP at the dot prompt and press Enter. A menu of help options appears on-screen.
2. Choose the command or function for which you need information.
3. To return to the dot prompt, press Esc.

From the Control Center

1. Position the highlight on one of the Control Center columns or a menu option.
2. To display the Help screen, press F1. Information about the currently selected item appears.
3. To view a list of other Help topics, choose Contents from the Help screen. To print the current topic, choose Print.
4. To return to the Control Center, press Esc.

Note

To get information about a particular command or function, type the command or function after the HELP command at the dot prompt.

IF/ENDIF

Purpose

Provides for conditional processing of program commands.

Command Syntax

```
IF <condition>
    <commands>
[ELSE
    <commands>]
ENDIF
```

From within a program

1. To perform a set of commands when a specified condition is met, use the IF/ENDIF command set. If the condition is evaluated to be false (.F.), the command(s) following the **IF** statement are not executed and, unless you use the ELSE statement, processing continues with the commands following the **ENDIF**.
2. To specify commands to be executed when the condition is not met, include the ELSE command line.

Note

Each **IF** construct must end with an **ENDIF** command.

IMPORT

Purpose

Creates dBASE IV database files from datafiles used by other popular software packages. Imports data from RapidFile, dBASE II, Lotus 1-2-3, PFS:File, or Framework versions II, III, and IV.

Command Syntax

IMPORT FROM <*file-name*> [TYPE] RPD / DBASEII / WK1 / WKS / PFS / FW2 / FW3 / FW4

From the dot prompt

Issue the IMPORT FROM command, specifying the file name, including extension, and the type of file you are importing. A dBASE IV file is created with the same file name, but with the .DBF extension.

From the Control Center

1. Choose Import from the Tools menu.
2. Select the type of file you want to import, and press Enter.

Note

To add records to an existing dBASE IV file from another dBASE IV file or from files in various other formats, use the APPEND FROM command.

INDEX/REINDEX

Purpose

Creates an index based on a key field or expression, which enables records of a database file to be ordered by the key field or expression.

Command Syntax

INDEX ON *<key-expression>* **TO** *<index-file-name>*/**TAG** *<tag-name>* [OF *<multiple-index-file-name>*] [FOR *<condition>*] [UNIQUE] [DESCENDING]

INDEX ON *<key-expression>* **TO** *<index-file-name>* [UNIQUE]

REINDEX

From the dot prompt

1. Open the database file with the **USE** command.
2. To create an index, issue the **INDEX** command, and then specify a field or expression as the index key. You also can specify **UNIQUE** to include only the first of duplicate records in the index, or **DESCENDING** to index in reverse order.
3. To select records you want to index, specify a condition with the **FOR** clause.

From the Control Center

1. Select a file in the Data column. To display the data structure, press **Shift F2**.
2. To create an index tag for a field, type **Y** in the Index column for that field.

3. To create an index based on an expression or to choose other indexing options, choose Create New Index from the Organize menu.
4. Choose Save Changes and Exit from the Exit menu, or press Ctrl-End to return to the Control Center.

Notes

When an index is active, records appear to be in a sorted order, though the database file remains in natural order. Indexes speed record searches and are necessary to maintain links between related files.

To activate an index, use the USE, SET INDEX, or SET ORDER commands, or use the Organize menu in the Browse, Edit, and database design screens.

To rebuild an active index file, use REINDEX. If records change and, for some reason, the index is not updated properly, the **REINDEX** command enables you to update the index to match the database records.

INPUT

Purpose

Accepts data entry from the user in a program.

Command Syntax

INPUT [<*prompt*>] TO <*memvar*>

From the dot prompt

Issue the INPUT command with an optional prompt that must be a character expression, and then specify a memory variable to store the response. If the memory variable (<*memvar*>) does not exist, dBASE creates it. In this case, the type of variable (numeric, date, character, logical) is determined by the data you enter.

Type INPUT "Enter the beginning date" TO MFROM and press Enter. The text within the quotation marks appears on the next line, and the cursor waits for you to type a value.

Note

INPUT typically is used in dBASE IV programs. The **@...SAY**, **GET** command offers greater flexibility due to its optional formats and templates.

INSERT

Purpose

Adds to a database file at the current record location a new empty record.

Command Syntax

INSERT [BEFORE] [BLANK] /[NOORGANIZE]

From the dot prompt

1. Open a datafile with the USE command.
2. To position the record pointer to a record after which you want to insert a new record, use GOTO.

3. Issue the INSERT command.
4. The new blank record appears, enabling you to enter data. To save the data and return to the dot prompt, press Ctrl-End.

Notes

To place the new record before rather than after the current record, include the BEFORE clause in the INSERT command.

To prevent the new record from appearing for data entry, use the BLANK clause.

JOIN

Purpose

Merges records and fields from two database files to create a new database file.

Command Syntax

JOIN WITH <*alias*> TO <*file-name*> FOR <*condition*> [FIELDS <*field-list*>]

From the dot prompt

1. To open two datafiles in different work areas, issue the USE...IN command.
2. Issue the JOIN command, referencing the open file in the unselected work area by its alias name (this may be the same as the file name).

From the Control Center

1. Select the primary datafile in the Data column, press Enter.
2. Choose Use File, choose the <create> option in the Queries column, and then press Enter.
3. In the query design screen, choose the Add File to Query option from the Layout menu. Select the second datafile for your query.
4. Move the highlight to the key field in one of the file skeletons.
5. Choose the Create Link by Pointing option from the Layout menu. "LINK1" appears in the selected field.
6. To move the other file skeleton, press F3 or F4. Position the highlight in the key field and press Enter so that "LINK1" also appears in that field.
7. To add or remove fields from the view, highlight each field and press F5.
8. Choose Write View As Database File from the Layout menu.
9. Specify a file name for the new joined file. Choose Save Changes and Exit from the Exit menu.

Notes

You cannot use memo fields in a **JOIN**.

You also can use the SET FIELDS command to specify fields to include in the new database.

To link two database files without creating a new joined file, use the SET RELATION command or create a view query.

KEYBOARD

Purpose

Places characters in the type-ahead keyboard buffer. dBASE IV accepts the characters as if you typed them.

Command Syntax

KEYBOARD<*expC*> [CLEAR]

From the dot prompt

Specifying the characters to be placed into the keyboard buffer, issue the KEYBOARDcommand from the dot prompt or from within a program. The CLEARoption clears the keyboard buffer before it inserts the specified characters.

LABEL FORM

Purpose

Prints labels using a label format file.

Command Syntax

LABEL FORM<*label-file-name*>/ ?[<*scope*>] [FOR <*condition*>] [WHILE <*condition*>] [SAMPLE] [TO PRINTER/TO FILE <*file-name*>]

From the dot prompt

1. To define the label format, issue the CREATE LABEL command.
2. After you save the label format on disk, issue a LABEL FORM command.
3. To send the label to the printer, include the TO PRINT clause in the LABEL FORM command.

From the Control Center

1. Select a file in the Data column, press Enter, and then choose Use File.
2. Select in the Labels column a corresponding label format file, press Enter, and then choose Print Labels.

Note

To print a sample label to align label stock in the printer, use the SAMPLE option.

LIST/DISPLAY

Purpose

Displays on-screen information from a datafile, or optionally sends the data to a printer or disk file. **LIST** and **DISPLAY** are the same, except that **DISPLAY** displays data one screen at a time and after each screen, prompts the user to `Press any key to continue.`

Command Syntax

LIST/DISPLAY [[FIELDS] <*expression-list*>] [OFF] [<*scope*>] [FOR <*condition*>] [WHILE<*condition*>] [TO PRINTER/TO FILE <*file-name*>]

LIST/DISPLAY FILES [[LIKE] <*skeleton*>] [TO PRINTER/TO FILE <*file-name*>]

LIST/DISPLAY HISTORY [LAST <*expN*>] [TO PRINTER/TO FILE <*file-name*>]

LIST/DISPLAY MEMORY [TO PRINTER/TO FILE <*file-name*>]

LIST/DISPLAY STATUS [TO PRINTER/TO FILE <*file-name*>]

LIST/DISPLAY STRUCTURE [IN <*alias*>] [TO PRINTER/TO FILE <*file-name*>]

LIST/DISPLAY USERS

From the dot prompt

To list the contents of records on-screen, open a database file with the USE command. Issue the DISPLAY ALL or LIST ALL command. To suppress the display of record numbers, use the OFF clause.

To display various types of information, you can use alternate forms of the **LIST** command.

Command	Displays
LIST FILES	Directory of files
LIST HISTORY	Previous commands executed
LIST MEMORY	Memory usage and variables
LIST STATUS	Information about current database and dBASE IV session
LIST STRUCTURE	Database structure
LIST USERS	Users logged in on a network session

LOAD

Purpose

Loads a binary program file into memory.

Command Syntax

LOAD<*binary-file-name*>

From the dot prompt

To read the binary program from the disk, issue the LOADcommand.

Note

After the program is loaded into memory, run the program by issuing a CALLcommand, and then use the RELEASE MODULEcommand to remove it from memory.

LOCATE

Purpose

Searches the active database file for a record matching a specific condition.

Command Syntax

LOCATE[FOR <*condition*> [<*scope*>] [WHILE <*condition*>]

CONTINUE

From the dot prompt

1. Open the datafile with the USE command.
2. Issue a LOCATE command.
3. To locate the next record that matches the condition, issue the CONTINUE command.

From the Control Center

1. Select a file in the Data column and press F2 to display the data. Move the highlight to the field you want to search.
2. Choose Forward Search from the Go To menu.
3. Enter the search string and press Enter.
4. To search for the next matching record, press Shift-F4.

LOGOUT

Purpose

Logs a user out of the current session and sets up a new log-in screen.

Command Syntax

LOGOUT

From the dot prompt

To clear the screen and display the log-in screen, use the LOGOUT command in a program.

Note

To establish the log-in verification functions and set the user-access level, issue the PROTECT command when beginning the dBASE IV session.

MODIFY APPLICATION

See *CREATE APPLICATION.*

MODIFY COMMAND/FILE

Purpose

Enables you to write or change a dBASE IV program.

Command Syntax

MODIFY COMMAND/FILE <*file-name*>
[WINDOW <*window-name*>]

From the dot prompt

1. Issue MODIFY COMMAND from the dot prompt and press Enter.
2. Enter or edit commands or other text.
3. Press Ctrl-End or choose Save Changes and Exit from the Exit menu.
4. To run the program or procedure, issue the DO command from the dot prompt or from within another program.

From the Control Center

1. To create a new program file, choose <create> from the Applications panel, press Enter, and then choose dBASE Program.
2. To edit an existing file, choose the program (.PRG) file from the Applications column, press Enter, and then choose Modify Application.

Note

Unless you specify in the CONFIG.DB file an alternate word processing program, **MODIFY COMMAND** invokes the dBASE IV text editor.

MODIFY LABEL

See *CREATE/MODIFY LABEL.*

MODIFY QUERY/VIEW

See *CREATE/MODIFY QUERY/VIEW.*

MODIFY REPORT

See *CREATE/MODIFY REPORT.*

MODIFY SCREEN

See *CREATE/MODIFY SCREEN.*

MODIFY STRUCTURE

See *CREATE or MODIFY STRUCTURE.*

MOVE WINDOW

See *DEFINE WINDOW.*

NOTE

Purpose

Enables you to include comments within program source code files.

Command Syntax

NOTE *<text>*
* *<text>*
<command> && *<text>*

From within a program

Use the NOTE or * command before text that is a comment and not a command line to be executed. Use the && command before comments that appear after a command but on the same line as the command.

ON ERROR/ESCAPE/KEY

Purpose

Executes a specified command when an error occurs, or when you press Esc or other specified keys.

Command Syntax

ON ERROR[<*command*>]

ON ESCAPE[<*command*>]

ON KEY[LABEL <*key-label-name*>] [<*command*>]

From the dot prompt

1. To execute a command or procedure when an error occurs, include in a program the ON ERROR command.
2. To specify a command or procedure to be executed when the user presses Esc, use in a program the ON ESCAPE command.
3. To specify a command or procedure to be executed when the key represented by the <*key-label-name*> is pressed, include in a program the ON KEY command.

Note

The **ON** condition remains in effect until you cancel it by typing at the dot prompt ON ERROR/ ESCAPE/ KEY with no command parameter.

ON EXIT BAR/MENU/PAD/POPUP

Purpose

Specifies a command to be executed when a user exits a menu, menu bar, menu pad, or pop-up menu.

Command Syntax

ON EXIT BAR *<expN>* OF *<popup name>* [*<command>*]

ON EXIT MENU *<menu name>* [*<command>*]

ON EXIT PAD *<pad name>* OF *<menu name>* [*<command>*]

ON EXIT POPUP *<popup name>* [*<command>*]

From the dot prompt

After you create menus and pop-up menus in a program, to designate a command to execute when the user moves the cursor off certain bars or pads of a menu or pop-up menu, use the ON EXIT statements.

ON MENU/POPUP

Purpose

Executes a command when a user selects certain pads in a menu or certain bars in a pop-up menu.

Command Syntax

ON MENU *<menu name>* [*<command>*]

ON POPUP *<popup name>* [*<command>*]

From the dot prompt

To execute a command when the user selects pads or bars that do not have an **ON PAD** or **ON BAR** command assigned to them, use ON MENU/ON POPUP. If you do not include the <*command*> with the statement, the command assigned previously for the specified menu or popup is disabled.

ON MOUSE

Purpose

Specifies a command to be executed when a user clicks the left mouse button.

Command Syntax

ON MOUSE [<*command*>]

From the dot prompt

To detect in a program when the user clicks the left mouse button, use ON MOUSE. When the user releases the mouse button, the designated command executes.

ON PAD

Purpose

Executes a command when you select a menu pad.

Command Syntax

ON PAD<*pad-name*> OF<*menu-name*> [<*command*>]/[ACTIVATE POPUP <*popup name*>]

From the dot prompt

Define the menus and pads with the DEFINE MENU and DEFINE PADcommands in your program. To specify the command to be executed for each pad when it is selected, include the ON PADcommand line.

From the Control Center

To design menus, choose the Design menu in the Applications Generator, and then to specify the command associated with each item in the menu, choose the Change Action option from the Item menu.

ON PAGE

Purpose

Identifies a command to be executed when a specified line on a printed page is reached.

Command Syntax

ON PAGE[AT LINE <*expN*> <*commands*>]

From the dot prompt

To specify actions such as printing headers and footers or forcing page breaks in a printed report, include in a program the ON PAGEcommand.

To disengage the page handler, issue an ON PAGE command without the optional clauses.

ON READERROR

Purpose

Traps errors that occur during data entry.

Command Syntax

ON READERROR [<*commands*>]

From the dot prompt

Include the **ON READERROR** command in programs to specify a command or procedure to execute when invalid data is entered.

ON SELECTION BAR

Executes a command when the user chooses a bar in a pop-up menu.

Command Syntax

ON SELECTION BAR <*expN*> OF <*popup name*> [<*command*>]

From the dot prompt

To specify in a program a command to be executed when the user chooses a certain bar in a pop-up menu, use the ON SELECTION BAR statement.

ON SELECTION MENU

Purpose

Executes a command when the user selects a pad in a menu.

Command Syntax

ON SELECTION MENU<*menu name*> [<*command*>]

From the dot prompt

To specify a command to be executed when a user chooses pads in a specified menu that do not have an **ON SELECTION PAD** command assigned to them, issue the ON SELECTION MENUcommand.

ON SELECTION PAD

See *DEFINE MENU/DEFINE PAD.*

ON SELECTION POPUP

See *DEFINE POPUP.*

PACK

See *DELETE.*

PARAMETERS

Purpose

Specifies local variables used to pass data from a calling program to a procedure or to functions.

Command Syntax

PARAMETERS *<parameter-list>*

From within a program

In a program that includes a procedure or user-defined function that requires information from a calling procedure, include the PARAMETERS statement as the first executable command, or place it immediately following the **PROCEDURE** command or the **FUNCTION** command. Local variables created by the **PARAMETERS** command are discarded when control is returned to the calling program.

PLAY MACRO

Purpose

Executes a macro from the current macro library.

Command Syntax

PLAY MACRO *<macro-name>*

From the dot prompt

To execute a macro, include in a program the PLAY MACRO command. To read a macro file from disk into memory, issue the RESTORE MACROS command.

From the Control Center

1. Choose Macros from the Tools menu.
2. Choose Play from the Macros submenu, and then select the macro.

Notes

To display a menu of macros, press Shift-F10 from anywhere in dBASE IV.

To insert characters into the keyboard buffer as an alternative to using a macro, use in a program the KEYBOARD command.

PRINTJOB/ENDPRINTJOB

Purpose

Marks the start and end of a print job, initializes the printer, ejects the paper, and spools to disk output for multiple copies.

Command Syntax

```
PRINTJOB
    <commands>
ENDPRINTJOB
```

From within a program

Set in a program for the print job the values of system variables (_pscodes, _peject, _pcolno, _pecodes, and _pcopies). To identify commands that are part of a print job, include the PRINTJOB and ENDPRINTJOB statements.

From the Control Center

Select a file from the Reports column, press Enter, and then choose Print Report.

Notes

Because the report form file includes the **PRINTJOB** construct, you do not need to use the **PRINTJOB/ ENDPRINTJOB** commands if you use the REPORT FORM command.

Because dBASE IV does not allow nesting of print jobs, do not include a **PRINTJOB** command set within another print job.

PRIVATE/PUBLIC

Purpose

PRIVATE identifies local memory variables to be used in a lower-level program that may have the same name as public variables or variables used in the calling program.

PUBLIC identifies variables or arrays that can be changed during the current session by any dBASE IV program. Public variables are not released automatically when a program ends.

Command Syntax

PRIVATE ALL [LIKE/EXCEPT <*skeleton*>]

PRIVATE <*memvar-list*>

PUBLIC <*memory-variable-list*>/[ARRAY <*array-definition-list*>]

From the dot prompt

To specify local memory variables for a lower-level program that will not overwrite any variables of the same name in the calling program, use the PRIVATE command. To specify variables that may be used throughout the application, use the PUBLIC command.

PROCEDURE

Purpose

Identifies a subroutine in a program.

Command Syntax

PROCEDURE <*procedure-name*>

From within a program

To identify subroutines called by a main program, use the PROCEDURE command. To accept information from the calling program, include in a procedure the PARAMETERS command line. To mark the end of a procedure and to return control to the calling program, use the RETURN command. To execute a procedure, issue in a program the DO command.

Notes

You can specify a procedure file with the SET PROCEDURE command. A program or procedure file can contain a maximum of 963 procedures.

PROTECT

Purpose

Displays the Protect menu, which enables you to administer the following three types of security on a dBASE IV system:

Log-in	Controls access to dBASE IV with password protection.
File and Field Access	Establishes levels of access to datafiles.
Data Encryption	Provides for automatic encryption/decryption of data.

Command Syntax

PROTECT

From the dot prompt

To invoke the Protect menus, issue the PROTECT command. When prompted, enter an administrator password.

From the Control Center

Choose Protect Data from the Tools menu.

Note

After you establish security using PROTECT, you must supply the administrator password to change the security options.

See *PRIVATE*.

QUIT

Purpose

Closes all open files and ends the current dBASE IV session and returns you to the operating system.

Command Syntax

QUIT [WITH <*expN*>]

From the dot prompt

Type QUIT and press Enter.

From the Control Center

Choose the Quit to DOS option from the Exit menu.

Note

You can use the optional WITH clause to return an integer value to the calling program or operating system.

READ

Purpose

Accepts data from the user by activating all **@...GET** commands issued since you last issued the **CLEAR**, **CLEAR ALL**, **CLEAR GETS**, or **READ** command.

Command Syntax

READ [SAVE]

From the dot prompt

To specify data you want to accept from the user, use in a program one or more @...GET commands, and then use the READ command to activate the **@...GET** commands.

Note

If you do not want to clear the **GET**s, use the SAVE option. When you use this option, the next **READ** command processes the same set of **GET**s.

RECALL

Purpose

Removes the deletion flag for records in a database.

Command Syntax

RECALL [<*scope*>] [FOR <*condition*>]
[WHILE <*condition*>]

From the dot prompt

1. To recall a single record, open a database file with the USE command. To move to the record you want to recall, use the GOTO command.
2. Type RECALL and press Enter.
3. To recall all marked records in the database file, issue the RECALL ALL command.

From the Control Center

1. Select a file in the Data column, and press F2.
2. Move the highlight to a record in the database file you marked for deletion.
3. Choose Clear Deletion Mark from the Records menu, or press Ctrl-U.
4. To return to the Control Center, choose the Exit option from the Exit menu.

See *INDEX*.

RELEASE

Purpose

Removes memory variables, modules, menus, pop-up menus, screens, and windows from memory.

Command Syntax

RELEASE *<memvar-list>*

RELEASE ALL [LIKE/EXCEPT*<skeleton>*]

RELEASE MODULES [<*module-name-list*>]
/MENUS [<*menu-name-list*>]
/POPUPS [<*popup-name-list*>]
/SCREENS [<*screen-name-list*>]
/WINDOWS [<*window-name-list*>]

From the dot prompt

To specify memory variables to be removed from memory, issue the RELEASE command. To delete all memory variables from memory, use the RELEASE ALL command.

To free up memory used by menus, pop-up menus, screens, and windows, use RELEASE MENUS/POPUPS/SCREENS/WINDOWS. To remove a program from memory loaded with the **LOAD** command, issue the RELEASE MODULES command.

RENAME

Purpose

Changes the name of a disk file.

Command Syntax

RENAME <*old-file-name*> TO <*new-file-name*>

From the dot prompt

Issue the RENAME command.

From the Control Center

1. Choose the DOS Utilities from the Tools menu.
2. In the DOS Utilities window, select the file you want to rename.

3. Choose Rename from the Operations menu. When prompted, type in the new name for the file and press Enter.
4. Choose Exit to Control Center from the Exit menu.

REPLACE

Purpose

Changes the data in one or more fields for one or more records.

Command Syntax

REPLACE <*field-name*> WITH <*exp*> [ADDITIVE] [,<*field-name*> WITH <*exp*> [ADDITIVE]] [<*scope*>] [REINDEX] [FOR <*condition*>] [WHILE <*condition*>]

From the dot prompt

1. Open the datafile with the USE command.
2. Issue the REPLACE command, specifying the field name(s) and the values to be placed in those fields.
3. Optionally, specify a condition to select records to be replaced.

From the Control Center

1. Select a file in the Data column, press Enter, and choose Use File.

2. Choose the <create> option in the Queries column.
3. In the query design screen, type the filter conditions below the appropriate fields.
4. Choose Specify the Update Operation from the Update menu, and then choose Replace Values.
5. Type WITH, followed by the expression, below the field you want to replace.
6. Choose Perform the Update from the Update menu.
7. Choose Save Changes and Exit from the Exit menu.

Note

To rebuild the active index file after you make the replacements, use the REINDEX option.

REPLACE FROM ARRAY

Purpose

Replaces fields in database records with data stored in an array.

Command Syntax

REPLACE FROM ARRAY *<array-name>* [*<scope>*] [REINDEX] [FIELDS *<field list>*] [FOR *<condition>*] [WHILE *<condition>*]

From the dot prompt

1. Open the database file with the USE command.
2. Issue the REPLACE FROM ARRAY command. You optionally can specify the fields to be replaced with the **FIELDS** option or the records to be affected with the scope, **FOR** and **WHILE** clauses. The default scope is the current record only.

Note

To limit the active fields, you can use the SET FIELDS command.

REPORT FORM

Purpose

Prints a report file from the active database using a report form.

Command Syntax

REPORT FORM *<report-form-file-name>* /?
[PLAIN] [HEADING]*<expC>*] [NOEJECT]
[SUMMARY] [*<scope>*] [FOR *<condition>*]
[WHILE *<condition>*] [TO PRINTER/
TO FILE *<file-name>*]

From the dot prompt

1. Open with the USE command the database files required by the report format.
2. Issue the REPORT FORM command and press Enter. To send the report to the printer, include the TO PRINT clause, or to print the report to a disk file, use the TO FILE option.

From the Control Center

1. Select a file in the Data column and press **Enter**.
2. Select a file in the Reports column and press **Enter**.
3. Choose the Begin Printing option from the Print menu.

Notes

To limit the records printed on the report, use the **FOR**, **WHILE**, and scope clauses. To suppress a form-feed before the report, use the **NOEJECT** option with **TO PRINTER**.

To print only subtotal and totals with no detail lines, use the **SUMMARY** option.

RESET

Purpose

Resets the integrity tag from a file.

Command Syntax

RESET [IN <*alias*>]

From the dot prompt

1. Write a datafile processing program that includes the **BEGIN TRANSACTION**, **END TRANSACTION** command set. When the program is run and the transaction processing begins, an integrity tag is placed on the file.
2. To restore the database file to its pre-transaction state, use the **ROLLBACK** command.

3. If the **ROLLBACK** was unsuccessful, or if you do not want to perform a **ROLLBACK**, issue the RESET command line at the dot prompt to remove the integrity tag from the database file, making the file available for another transaction.

RESTORE

Purpose

Retrieves and activates memory variables, macros, and windows from disk files, or screen images from memory.

Command Syntax

RESTORE FROM *<file-name>* [ADDITIVE]

RESTORE MACROS FROM *<macro-file>*

RESTORE SCREEN FROM *<screen-name>*

RESTORE WINDOW *<window-name-list>/* ALL FROM *<file-name>*

From the dot prompt

1. To save memory variables to a file, use the SAVE TO *<file-name>* command. To restore variables to a file, use the RESTORE FROM *<file-name>* command.
2. To load a macro library from disk into memory, issue the RESTORE MACROS command.
3. To load a window definition into memory from a disk file, use the RESTORE WINDOW command.
4. To replace the current screen image with one stored in memory, issue the RESTORE SCREEN FROM command.

From the Control Center

1. To access a macro library, choose Macros from the Tool menu.
2. Choose Load Library from the Macros submenu.

RESUME

Purpose

Resumes execution of a suspended program.

Command Syntax

RESUME

From the dot prompt

1. To stop a program temporarily, include the SUSPEND command in a program, and then execute the program.
2. When the program is suspended, use the RESUME command from the dot prompt to continue execution of the program at the command line following the SUSPEND command.

RETRY

Purpose

Re-executes a command that has caused an error.

Command Syntax

RETRY

From the dot prompt

Include the ON ERROR DO <*procedure*> WITH ERROR( ) command to handle errors encountered in a program. To instruct dBASE IV to re-execute the command that caused the error, include the RETRY command in the error-handling procedure.

RETURN

Purpose

Restores control to a calling program.

Command Syntax

RETURN [<*expression*> / TO MASTER/TO <*procedure*>]

From within a program

To return control to the calling program or procedure, place the RETURN command at the end of a procedure or user-defined function.

Notes

When you include the TO MASTER clause, processing continues with the highest-level calling program.

To return a value from a user-defined function, include the <*expression*> after the RETURN statement.

ROLLBACK

See *BEGIN/END TRANSACTION.*

RUN/!

Purpose

Executes a DOS program or command.

Command Syntax

RUN *<DOS-command>*

! *<DOS-command>*

From the dot prompt

To run a DOS command or external program from within dBASE IV, issue the RUN or ! command.

From the Control Center

1. Choose DOS Utilities from the Tools menu.
2. To execute a DOS command, choose the Perform DOS command option from the DOS menu.
3. To go to a DOS prompt screen, choose the Go to DOS option from the DOS menu. To return to dBASE IV, type EXIT and press Enter.

Notes

You should run memory-resident commands such as **ASSIGN** or **PRINT** prior to loading dBASE IV. Be sure you have enough memory available for the DOS

COMMAND.COM program, as well as the program you will be running when using **RUN**. To roll dBASE IV out of memory while running an external program, use the RUN( ) function.

SAVE

Purpose

Saves memory variables, macros, and windows to disk, and saves screen images to memory.

Command Syntax

SAVE TO *<file-name>* [ALL LIKE/EXCEPT *<skeleton>*]

SAVE MACROS TO *<macro-file>*

SAVE SCREEN TO *<screen name>*

SAVE WINDOW *<window-name-list>*/ ALL TO *<file-name>*

From the dot prompt

1. Create the memory variables, macros, windows, or screen images.
2. To save the information on disk, use a SAVE command; or to save the screen image in memory, use the SAVE SCREEN command.

From the Control Center

1. Create the macros you want to save to disk.
2. Choose Macros from the Tools menu. To write the current macros to the disk, choose the Save Library option from the Macros submenu.

Note

To retrieve variables and objects you saved with the **SAVE** commands, use the RESTORE commands.

SCAN/ENDSCAN

Purpose

Performs a set of commands repeatedly as needed for processing records in a database file.

Command Syntax

```
SCAN [<scope>] [FOR <condition>]
[WHILE<condition>]
    [<commands>...]
    [LOOP]
    [EXIT]
ENDSCAN
```

From within a program

To create a programming construct to process records in a database, use the SCAN and ENDSCAN commands. Mark the beginning of the construct with the SCAN command and end the construct with the ENDSCAN command.

Note

The **SCAN/ENDSCAN** command set is similar to the **DO WHILE/ENDDO** command set; however, because the **SKIP** is implicit in the **SCAN/ENDSCAN** construct, the **SKIP** command is not required with **SCAN/ENDSCAN** to move to each record.

SEEK

Purpose

Performs a search for a record matching a specified value in an indexed database file.

Command Syntax

SEEK <*expression*>

From the dot prompt

1. Open the database and index files with the USE command, specifying the key field with the ORDER option.
2. To find a record with a matching value in the key field, issue a SEEK command with an expression.

From the Control Center

1. Select a file from the Data column and press F2 to display the data.
2. Position the cursor in the field you want to search. If an index for that field is not active, choose Order Records by Index from the Organize menu.
3. Choose Index Key Search from the Go To menu. When prompted, type in the value for which you want to search, and then press Enter.

Note

If you do not find an exact match with **SEEK**, you can instruct dBASE IV to move to the record with the nearest value by using the SET NEAR ON command.

SELECT

Purpose

Chooses a work area in which to open or use a database file.

Command Syntax

SELECT <*work-area-name/alias*>

From the dot prompt

1. Open a database file in work area 1 with the USE command.
2. To access work area 2, type SELECT 2 and then press Enter.
3. Open another database file.
4. To return to work area 1, type SELECT 1 and press Enter.

Notes

An alternative to **SELECT** is the **IN** clause, which is available with some commands. To specify that you want to open the **NAMES.DBF** file in work area 3, for example, issue the command USE NAMES IN 3.

dBASE IV 2.0 allows you to access a maximum of 40 work areas. You can reference work areas by an alias name, the number of the work area, or using letters **A** through **J** for work areas 1 through 10.

SET

Purpose

Enables you to change various dBASE IV environment settings.

Command Syntax

SET

From the dot prompt

1. To access a menu of various settings available, type SET and press Enter.
2. Choose the options you want, and then press Ctrl-End to save your changes and return to the dot prompt.
3. To change a particular setting, issue the appropriate SET command from the dot prompt or from within a program.

From the Control Center

1. Choose Settings from the Tools menu.
2. Choose the options you want, and then choose Exit to Control Center from the Exit menu.

The default settings in the following list of **SET** commands appear in uppercase letters

SET ALTERNATE on/OFF

SET ALTERNATE TO [<*file-name*> [ADDITIVE]]

SET AUTOSAVE on/OFF

SET BELL ON/off

SET BELL TO [<*frequency*>,<*duration*>]

SET BLOCKSIZE TO *<expN>*

SET BORDER TO [SINGLE/DOUBLE/PANEL/ NONE/*<definition>*]

SET CARRY on/**OFF**

SET CARRY TO [*<field-name-list>* [ADDITIVE]]

SET CATALOG on/**OFF**

SET CATALOG TO [*<file-name>/?*]

SET CENTURY on/**OFF**

SET CLOCK on/**OFF**

SET CLOCK TO [*<row>,<column>*]

SET COLOR ON/OFF

SET COLOR TO [*<standard>*] [, [*<enhanced>*] [, [<perimeter>] [, [<background>]]]]

SET COLOR OF NORMAL/MESSAGES/TITLES/ BOX/HIGHLIGHT/INFORMATION/FIELDS TO [*<attribute>*]

SET CONFIRM on/**OFF**

SET CONSOLE ON/off

SET CURRENCY TO [*<expC>*]

SET CURRENCY LEFT/right

SET CURSOR ON/off

SET DATE [TO] **AMERICAN**/*ansi/british/french/ german/italian/japan/usa/mdy/dmy/ymd*

SET DBTRAP ON/off

SET DEBUG on/**OFF**

SET DECIMALS TO *<expN>*

SET DEFAULT TO [*<drive>* [:]]

SET DELETED on/**OFF**

SET DELIMITERS on/**OFF**

SET DELIMITERS TO [*<expC>*/DEFAULT]

SET DESIGN ON/off

SET DEVELOPMENT ON/off

SET DEVICE TO SCREEN/*printer*/*file* *<file-name>*

SET DIRECTORY TO [[*<drive>*] [*<path>*]]

SET DISPLAY TO MONO/COLOR/EGA25/ EGA43/MONO43/VGA25/VGA43/VGA50

SET ECHO on/OFF

SET ENCRYPTION ON/off

SET ESCAPE ON/off

SET EXACT on/OFF

SET EXCLUSIVE on/OFF

SET FIELDS on/OFF

SET FIELDS TO [*<field>* [/R]/ *<calculated- field>*...] [, *<field>* [/R]/ *<calculated-field>*...]

SET FIELDS TO ALL [LIKE/*except* *<skeleton>*]

SET FILTER TO [FILE *<file-name>*/?]/ [*<condition>*]

SET FORMAT TO [*<format-file-name>*/?]

SET FULLPATH on/OFF

SET FUNCTION *<expN>*/*<expC>*/*<key label>* TO *<expC>*

SET HEADINGS ON/off

SET HELP ON/off

SET HISTORY ON/off

SET HISTORY TO *<expN>*

SET HOURS TO [12/24]

SET IBLOCK TO *<expN>*

SET INDEX TO ?

SET INDEX TO *<index-file-name-list>* [ORDER *<index-file-name>*]

SET INDEX TO *<multiple-index-file-name-list>* [ORDER *<multiple-index-tag>* [OF *<multiple-index-file-name>*]]

SET INSTRUCT ON/off

SET INTENSITY ON/off

SET KEY TO [*<exp-match>* /RANGE *<exp-low>*,*<exp-high>*/*<exp-low>*[,]/,*<exp-high>*] [IN *<alias>*]

SET LDCHECK ON/off

SET LIBRARY TO [*<file-name>*]

SET LOCK ON/off

SET MARGIN TO *<expN>*

SET MARK TO [*<expC>*]

SET MBLOCK TO *<expN>*

SET MEMOWIDTH TO *<expN>*

SET MESSAGE TO [*<expC>* [AT *<expN>*[,*<expN>*]]]

SET MOUSE ON/off

SET NEAR on/OFF

SET ODOMETER TO *<expN>*

SET ORDER TO

SET ORDER TO *<expN>*

SET ORDER TO *<index-file>*/[TAG] *<tag-name>* [OF *<multiple-index-file>*] [NOSAVE]

SET PATH TO [*<path-list>*]

SET PAUSE on/OFF

SET POINT TO [*<expC>*]

SET PRECISION TO [*<expN>*]

SET PRINTER on/OFF

SET PRINTER TO *<DOS-device>*

SET PRINTER TO *<computer-name>**<printer-name>* = *<destination>*

SET PRINTER TO \\SPOOLER

SET PRINTER TO \\CAPTURE

SET PRINTER TO FILE *<file-name>*

SET PROCEDURE TO [*<procedure-file-name>*]

SET REFRESH TO *<expN>*

SET RELATION TO [*<expression>* INTO *<alias>* [, *<expression>* INTO *<alias>* ...]]

SET REPROCESS TO *<expN>*

SET SAFETY ON/off

SET SCOREBOARD ON/off

SET SEPARATOR TO [*<expC>*]

SET SKIP TO [*<alias>* [, *<alias>*]...]

SET SPACE ON/off

SET SQL on/OFF

SET STATUS on/OFF

SET STEP on/OFF

SET TALK ON/off

SET TITLE ON/off

SET TRAP on/OFF

SET TYPEAHEAD TO *<expN>*

SET UNIQUE on/OFF

SET VIEW TO *<query-file-name>*/*<view-file-name>*/?

SET WINDOW OF MEMO TO *<window-name>*

SHOW MENU

See *DEFINE MENU.*

SHOW POPUP

See *DEFINE POPUP.*

SKIP

Purpose

Moves the current record pointer in a database forwards or backwards.

Command Syntax

SKIP [*<expN>*] [IN *<alias>*]

From the dot prompt

To move the record pointer, use the SKIP command at the dot prompt or in a program. If the command is used with no numeric expression, the record pointer moves forward one record. To specify the number of records to move the pointer forward, include a positive number; or to specify the number of records to move the pointer backwards, include a negative number.

From the Control Center

1. Select a file name in the Data column, and press F2 to display the data.
2. Select Skip from the Go To menu. Enter at the prompt the number of records you want to skip.

SORT

Purpose

Creates a new a database file in which the records of the active database are positioned in sorted order.

Command Syntax

SORT TO <*file-name*> ON <*field-1*> [/A] [/C] [/D] [, <*field-2*> [/A] [/C] [/D]...] [ASCENDING/ DESCENDING] [<*scope*>] [FOR <*condition*>] [WHILE <*condition*>]

From the dot prompt

1. Open a database file with the USE command.
2. Issue the SORT TO command, specifying the name of the new file to hold the sorted records.

From the Control Center

1. Select a file in the Data column, and press Shift-F2 to display the data structure.
2. Choose the Sort Database on Field List option from the Organize submenu.

Notes

You cannot sort logical or memo fields. To disregard case when sorting, use the /C option. To sort in reverse order, use the DESCENDING or /D option.

STORE

Purpose

Creates a new memory variable or saves a value to an existing memory variable or array element.

Command Syntax

STORE *<expression>* TO *<memvar-list>*
 /<array-element-list>
<memvar>/<array-element> = *<expression>*

From the dot prompt

To create a memory variable or assign a new value to a variable, use the STORE (or =) command at the dot prompt or within a program

Note

Memory variable names can be a maximum of 10 characters long and must begin with a letter. The data type of the memory variable is determined by the type of data assigned to the variable.

SUM

See *CALCULATE*.

SUSPEND

Purpose

Suspends execution of a dBASE IV program. This command is useful when debugging programs.

Command Syntax

SUSPEND

From the dot prompt

1. To stop a program temporarily, include the SUSPEND command in the program. You return to the dot prompt, where you can display or change memory variables or records.
2. To resume execution of the program with the next command line after the **SUSPEND** command, issue RESUME command; or to cancel the program and remove it from memory, use the CANCEL command.

TEXT, ENDTEXT

Purpose

Prints a block of text to the screen, printer, or a file.

Command Syntax

TEXT
[<*text-characters*>]
ENDTEXT

From the dot prompt

1. To mark the beginning of a text block, place the TEXT command on a line by itself in a program file.
2. Type on the line following the **TEXT** command one or more lines of text you want to print.
3. Follow on a line by itself the text with the ENDTEXT command.

Notes

To send text to the printer, use the SET PRINTER ON command. To open a disk file to receive the text output, use the SET ALTERNATE ON command.

TOTAL

Purpose

Sums numeric fields of the active database and creates a second database file in which to store the results. The numeric fields in the new database contain the totals for all records with the same key value in the original database file.

Command Syntax

TOTAL ON *<key-field>* TO *<file-name>* [FIELDS *<field-list>*] [*<scope>*] [FOR *<condition>*] [WHILE *<condition>*]

From the dot prompt

1. To open a database file containing at least one numeric field, issue the USE command.

2. If the database currently is not indexed or sorted on the key field, do this with the INDEX or SORT commands.
3. Issue the TOTAL command, specifying the key field.

TYPE

Purpose

Displays the contents of a text file.

Command Syntax

TYPE <*file-name*> [TO PRINTER/TO FILE <*file-name*>] [NUMBER]

From the dot prompt

To display the contents of the file on the screen, or optionally send the text to the printer or to another file, issue with the file name the TYPE command. To add line numbers at the beginning of each line of text, include the NUMBER option.

From the Control Center

1. Choose DOS Utilities from the Tools menu.
2. Select the file you want to display in the DOS Utilities window.
3. To display the text, choose View from the Operations menu.

UNLOCK

Purpose

Releases file locks so that other users can modify records.

Command Syntax

UNLOCK [ALL/IN <*alias*>]

From the dot prompt

With an open database locked with the **FLOCK( )** function, or in a record locked with **RLOCK( )**, make necessary record changes, and then release the locking by issuing the UNLOCK command. This enables other users in a multi-user environment to modify the file.

UPDATE

Purpose

Uses data from another database to update fields in the current database by matching records on a key field.

Command Syntax

UPDATE ON <*key-field*> FROM <*alias*>
REPLACE <*field-1*> WITH <*expression-1*>
[,<*field-2*> WITH <*expression-2*>...] [RANDOM]
[REINDEX]

From the dot prompt

To open the database files in separate work areas, issue the USE...IN command. Issue the UPDATE command, referencing the source database by alias name.

From the Control Center

1. Choose <create> in the Queries column.
2. To place file skeletons on the query design surface, choose Add File to Query from the Layout menu. To link the files, use the Create Link by Pointing option from the Layout menu.
3. Select the field you want to update, and then choose Specify Update Operation/Replace Values in <*filename*> from the Update menu.
4. Choose Perform the Update from the Update menu.

Note

Both files you use with the **UPDATE** command must be indexed on the key field, unless you specify the **RANDOM** option.

Purpose

Opens an existing database file, as well as the appropriate index and memo files.

Command Syntax

USE [<*file-name*>/?] [IN < *-area-number*>] [INDEX <*index-file-list/multiple-index-file*>] [ORDER <*index-file-name*/[[TAG] < *tag-name*> [OF <*multiple-index-file-name*>]]] [ALIAS <*alias*>] [EXCLUSIVE] [NOUPDATE] [NOLOG] [NOSAVE] [AGAIN]

From the dot prompt

To open a database file name, issue the USE command. To open a database in another work area, use the IN option. To close the active database file issue the USE command by itself with no file name.

From the Control Center

Select a file in the Data column, press Enter, and then choose Use File.

WAIT

Purpose

Pauses program execution until the user presses a key.

Command Syntax

WAIT [<*prompt*>] [TO <*memvar*>]

From the dot prompt

To prompt the user to press a key to continue, use the WAIT command in a program. To store the keypress to a memory variable, use the TO option.

Note

The **@...GET** command provides greater flexibility in accepting user input due to its optional formats and templates.

ZAP

Purpose

Removes all records in a database file.

Command Syntax

ZAP

From the dot prompt

To permanently remove all records from the active database file, issue the ZAP command. If **SET SAFETY** is **ON**, you are prompted to confirm the removal of records. To proceed with the deletion of the records, press Y for Yes.

dBASE IV FUNCTIONS

& *<character-variable>* [.]
Macro substitution.

ABS(*<expN>*)
Returns absolute value.

ACCESS( )
Returns the access level of the current user.

ACOS(*<expN>*)
Returns angle size in radians of a cosine.

ALIAS([*<expN>*])
Returns the alias name of a work area.

ASC(*<expC>*)
Returns ASCII decimal code for first character of a string.

ASIN(*<expN>*)
Returns the angle size in radians of a sine.

AT(*<expC-1>*, *<expC-2>*/*<memo>* [,*<expN>*])
Returns location of a string a character expression or memo field.

ATAN(*<expN>*)
Returns the angle size in radians of a tangent.

ATN2(*<expN-1>*,*<expN-2>*)
Returns the angle size in radians of a sine and cosine.

BAR()
Returns the number of the last selected prompt bar from the active pop-up menu.

BARCOUNT([*<expC>*])
Returns the number of bars in pop-up menu.

BARPROMPT(*<expN>*[,*<expC>*])
Returns text in a bar of a pop-up menu.

BOF([*<alias>*])
Returns `.T.` if at beginning of file.

CALL(*<expC>*,*<expression>*, [*<expression-list>*])
Executes a `LOAD`ed binary program module.

CATALOG()
Returns the active catalog file name.

CDOW(*<expD>*)
Returns the name of the day of the week.

CEILING(*<expN>*)
Returns the smallest integer >= to a value.

CERROR()
Returns the number of the last compiler error message.

CHANGE ([*<alias>*])
Determines if a record has been changed by a network user.

CHR(*<expN>*)
Converts numeric expression to character.

CMONTH(*<expD>*)
Returns the name of the month from a date.

COL()
Returns the cursor column position on-screen.

COMPLETED()
Returns `.T.` if a transaction is complete.

COS(*<expN>*)
Returns the cosine value of an angle in radians.

CTOD(*<expC>*)
Converts from date to character.

DATE( )
Returns the system date.

DAY(*<expD>*)
Returns the day of month from a date.

DBF([*<alias>*])
Returns the name of the database in use.

DELETED([*<alias>*])
Returns `.T.` if current record is marked for deletion.

DESCENDING([[*<multiple-index-file>*,] *<expN>* [,*<alias>*]])
Returns `.T.` if index tag is created with the `DESCENDING` option.

DGEN(*<expC1>* [, *<expC2>*])
Runs a template language program.

DIFFERENCE(*<expC>*,*<expC>*)
Returns the difference between two `SOUNDEX( )` codes.

DISKSPACE( )
Returns number of free bytes on the default drive.

DMY(*<expD>*)
Converts a date to DD Month YY form.

DOW(*<expD>*)
Returns the number of the day of the week from a date.

DTOC(*<expD>*)
Converts a date to a character expression.

DTOR(*<expN>*)
Converts angle size in degrees to radians.

DTOS(*<expD>*)
Converts date to a character expression in the form CCYYMMDD.

EOF([*<alias>*])
Returns `.T.` if at the end of file.

ERROR( )
Returns the last error number.

EXP(*<expN>*)
Returns value of *e* raised to *<expN>*.

FDATE(*<expC>*)
Returns date a file was last modified.

FIELD(*<expN>*[, *<alias>*])
Returns field name corresponding to a field number.

FILE(*<expC>*)
Verifies the existence of a file.

FIXED(*<expN>*)
Converts a floating point number to a binary coded decimal.

FKLABEL(*<expN>*)
Returns the name of a function key from its number.

FKMAX( )
Returns the maximum number of programmable function keys.

FLDCOUNT([*<alias>*]
Returns the number of fields in a database structure.

FLDLIST([*<expN>*]
Returns *n*th field of a SET FIELDS list.

FLOAT(*<expN>*)
Converts binary coded decimal numbers to floating point.

FLOCK([*<alias>*])
Locks a database file.

FLOOR(<*expN*>)
Returns the largest integer <= to a value.

FOR([[<*multiple-index-file*>,]<*expN*>[,<*alias*>]])
Returns FOR condition used for an index tag.

FOUND([<*alias*>])
Returns .T. if record is found with SEEK, FIND, LOCATE, or CONTINUE.

FSIZE(<*expC*>)
Returns the size of file in bytes.

FTIME(<*expC*>)
Returns the time a file was last modified.

FV(<*payment*>,<*rate*>,<*periods*>)
Returns the future value of investment at fixed interest for a given of time periods.

GETENV(<*expC*>)
Returns the contents of a DOS environment variable.

HOME()
Returns the path from which dBASE was run.

ID()
Returns the name of the current user on the network.

IIF(<*condition*>,<*exp-1*>,<*exp-2*>)
Immediate If, returns first expression if .T., otherwise returns second expression.

INKEY([*expN*])
Returns the decimal ASCII value of the last key pressed.

INT(<*expN*>)
Converts a number to an integer.

ISALPHA(<*expC*>)
Returns .T. if the expression begins with an alphabetic character.

ISBLANK(<*exp*>)
Returns .T. if an expression is blank.

ISCOLOR( )
Returns .T. if system has color capability.

ISLOWER(<*expC*>)
Returns .T. if first character is lowercase.

ISMARKED([<*alias*>])
Returns .T. if a record is changed during transaction.

ISMOUSE( )
Indicates if a mouse driver is installed.

ISUPPER(<*expC*>)
Returns .T. if the first character is uppercase.

KEY([[<*multiple-index-file*>,] <*expN*> [,<*alias*>]])
Returns a key expression for the specified index file.

KEYMATCH(<*exp*> [,<*index number*> [,<*work-area*>]])
Indicates if an expression is found in index.

LASTKEY( )
Returns the decimal ASCII value of the key pressed to exit full-screen command.

LEFT(<*expC*>/<*memo*>,<*expN*>)
Returns a specified number of characters counting from the left of a string.

LEN(<*expC*>/<*memo*>)
Returns the number of characters in a specified string or a memo field.

LIKE(<*pattern*>,<*expC*>)
Compares strings. May contain wild-card characters.

LINENO( )
Returns the line number to be executed next in the current program.

LKSYS(<*expN*>)
Returns the time, date, and log-in name for a locked file.

LOCK([*<expC-list>*,*<alias>*] /[,*<alias>*])
Locks a datafile record in the network system. See also *RLOCK*.

LOG(*<expN>*)
Returns the natural logarithm of a number.

LOG10(*<expN>*)
Returns the logarithm to base 10.

LOOKUP(*<return-exp>*,*<look-for-exp>*,*<look-in-field>*)
Looks up a record from a specified database file.

LOWER(*<expC>*)
Converts uppercase letters to lowercase.

LTRIM(*<expC>*)
Removes leading blanks from a character string.

LUPDATE([*<alias>*])
Returns the last date of file update of a specified database file.

MAX(*<exp-1>*,*<exp-2>*)
Returns the greater of two values.

MCOL( )
Returns column position of the mouse pointer.

MDX([*<expN>*[,*<alias>*]])
Returns the name of an open .MDX file.

MDY(*<expD>*)
Converts the date format to month DD, YY.

MEMLINES(*<memo-field-name>*)
Returns at the current width the number of word-wrapped lines in a memo field.

MEMORY([*<expN>*])
Returns the amount of RAM in kilobytes available in or allocated to various memory regions.

MENU()
Returns the name of the active menu.

MESSAGE()
Returns the last error message.

MIN(*<exp-1>*,*<exp-2>*)
Returns the lesser of two values.

MLINE(*<memo-field-name>*,*<expN>*)
Returns a line of a memo field.

MOD(*<expN-1>*,*<expN-2>*)
Returns the remainder from a division of two numbers.

MONTH(*<expD>*)
Returns the number of the month from a date.

MROW()
Returns the row position of the mouse pointer.

NDX([*<expN>* [,*<alias>*]])
Returns name of an open .NDX file.

NETWORK()
Determines if dBASE IV is running on a network.

ORDER([*<alias>*])
Returns the name of primary order index file or .MDX tag.

OS()
Returns name of the operating system.

PAD()
Returns the prompt pad name from the active menu.

PADPROMPT(*<expC1>* [,*<expC2>*])
Returns text in a pad of a menu.

PAYMENT(*<principal>*,*<rate>*,*<periods>*)
Calculates periodic payment on a loan with a fixed interest.

PCOL( )
Returns the printer column position.

PCOUNT( )
Returns the number of parameters passed to a procedure or function.

PI( )
Returns the mathematical constant for the ratio of circumference to diameter.

POPUP( )
Returns the name of the active pop-up menu.

PRINTSTATUS( )
Returns `.T.` if the printer is ready.

PROGRAM( )
Returns the name of program being executed.

PROMPT( )
Returns the prompt of the last-selected pop-up or menu option.

PROW( )
Returns the printer row position.

PV(*<payment>*,*<rate>*,*<periods>*)
Calculates the present value of equal payments invested at fixed interest for a certain number of payment periods.

RAND([*<expN>*])
Generates a random number.

RAT(*<expC1>*,*<expC2>*/*<memo-field>*[,*<expN>*])
Returns position of a character string in another string, counting from the right.

READKEY( )
Returns the value of the key pressed to exit full screen.

RECCOUNT([*<alias>*])
Returns the number of records in the database file.

RECNO([*<alias>*])
Returns the current record number in the database file.

RECSIZE([*<alias>*])
Returns the size of a record in a database file.

REPLICATE(*<expC>*,*<expN>*)
Repeats a character expression a specified number of times.

RIGHT(*<expC>*/*<memo-field>*,*<expN>*)
Returns a specified number of characters, counting from the right.

RLOCK([*<expC-list>*,*<alias>*] /[,*<alias>*])
Locks one or more database records.

ROLLBACK( )
Determines if the most recent rollback was successful.

ROUND(*<expN-1>*,*<expN-2>*)
Rounds the number in *<expN-1>* to *<expN-2>* decimal places.

ROW( )
Returns the row number of the current cursor position.

RTOD(*<expN>*)
Converts radians to degrees.

RTRIM(*<expC>*)
Removes trailing blanks. See also *TRIM*( ).

RUN([*<expL1>*,] *<expC>*[,*<expL2>*])
Executes an operating system command or program and returns a completion code.

SEEK(*<expC>* [,*<alias>*])
Searches indexed database files.

SELECT([*<alias>*]
Returns the number of available work areas or the work area number of a specified alias.

SET(<*expC*>)
Returns the current settings of a **SET** command.

SIGN(<*expN*>)
Returns a mathematical sign of a numeric expression.

SIN(<*expN*>)
Returns a sine from an angle in radians.

SOUNDEX(<*expC*>)
Returns the four-character soundex code.

SPACE(<*expN*>)
Generates a character string of blank spaces.

SQRT(<*expN*>)
Returns the square root of a specified number.

STR(<*expN*> [,<*length*> [,<*decimal*>]])
Converts a number to a character string.

STUFF(<*expC-1*>,<*expN-1*>,<*expN-2*>,<*expC-2*>)
Replaces the part of a character string with another character string.

SUBSTR(<*expC*>/<*memo-field name*>,<*starting-position*> [,<*number-of-characters*>])
Extracts a specified number or characters from a string or memo field.

TAG([[<*multiple-index-file*>,] <*expN*>[,<*alias*>]])
Returns the tag name in a specified .MDX file.

TAGCOUNT([<*multiple-index-file*> [,<*alias*>]])
Returns the number of active indexes.

TAGNO([<*order-name*> [,<*multiple-index-name*> [,<*alias*>]]])
Returns the index tag number.

TAN(<*expN*>)
Returns the tangent of an angle in radians.

TIME([<*exp*>])
Returns system time.

TRANSFORM(*<exp>*,*<expC>*)
Returns picture formatting of character, logical, date, and numeric data without using the **@...SAY** commands.

TRIM(*<expC>*)
Removes trailing blanks.

TYPE(*<expC>*)
Returns an uppercase letter (`C`, `N`, `L`, `M`, `D`, `F`, or `U`) representing data type of an evaluated expression.

UNIQUE([[*<expC>*,] *<expN>* [,*<alias>*]])
Returns `.T.` if an index tag was created using the **UNIQUE** option.

UPPER(*<expC>*)
Converts lowercase letters to uppercase.

USER()
Returns the log-in name of the network user.

VAL(*<expC>*)
Converts characters to numbers.

VARREAD()
Returns the name of a field or variable being edited.

VERSION()
Returns the dBASE IV version number in use.

WINDOW()
Returns the name of the active window.

YEAR(*<expD>*)
Returns the year from date expression.

LOW-LEVEL FILE I/O FUNCTIONS

Low-level file I/O functions enable dBASE IV programmers to manipulate operating system level binary files. These functions are similar to C language file functions. They work with data stream files at the operating system level and require a knowledge of programming at that level.

FCLOSE(*<expN>*)
Closes a low-level file.

FCREATE(*<expC-1>* [,*<expC-2>*])
Creates and opens a low-level file.

FEOF(*<expN>*)
Returns the end of file status.

FERROR( )
Returns the error status number of a low-level file operation.

FFLUSH(*<expN>*)
Writes system buffer of a low-level file to disk.

FGETS(*<expN-1>* [,*<expN-2>*] [,*<expC>*])
Reads a character string from a low-level file.

FOPEN(*<expC-1>* [,*<expC-2>*])
Opens a low-level file.

FPUTS(*<expN-1>*,*<expC-1>* [,*<expN-2>*]
[,*<expC-2>*])
Writes a character string to a low-level file.

FREAD(*<expN-1>*,*<expN-2>*)
Reads bytes from a low-level file.

FSEEK(*<expN-1>*,*<expN-2>* [,*<expN-3>*])
Moves the file pointer in a low-level file.

FWRITE(*<expN-1>*,*<expC-1>* [,*<expN-2>*])
Writes characters to a low-level file.

SYSTEM MEMORY VARIABLES

dBASE IV provides several predefined system memory variables with default values that control printer parameters and the appearance of printed output. You can change the settings of these system variables at the dot prompt or from within a program. The default values for the system variables in the following syntax descriptions are printed first in uppercase.

_ALIGNMENT = "LEFT"/"center"/"right"
Alignment of output.

_BOX = T./.f.
Specifies whether boxes print.

_INDENT = *<expN>*
Indention for the first line of each paragraph.

_LMARGIN = *<expN>*
Page left margin (0 to 254).

_PADVANCE = "FORMFEED"/"linefeeds"
Advances paper.

_PAGENO = *<expN>*
Current page number (1 to 32,767).

_PBPAGE = *<expN>*
Starts print job at specified page number (1 to 32,767).

_PCOLNO = *<expN>*
Printer column number (0 to 255).

_PCOPIES = *<expN>*
Number of copies to be printed (1 to 32,767).

_PDRIVER = "*<file-name>*"
Printer driver.

_PECODE = *<expC>*
Ending control codes for print job.

_PEJECT = **"BEFORE"/"after"/"both"/"none"**
When to eject page.

_PEPAGE = *<expN>*
Ends print job at page number (1 to 32,767).

_PFORM = "*<file-name>*"
Prints form file, containing all system memory variable settings.

_PLENGTH = *<expN>*
Printed page length (1 to 32,767).

_PLINENO = *<expN>*
Line number on page (0 or any integer less than _plength).

_PLOFFSET = *<expN>*
Page left offset for printed output (0 to 254).

_PPITCH = **"DEFAULT"/"pica"/"elite"/ "condensed"**
Printer pitch.

_PQUALITY = **.F./.t.**
Letter quality (`.T.`) or draft (`.F.`) mode.

_PSCODE = *<expC>*
Starting control codes for a print job.

_PSPACING = **1/2/3**
Line spacing for printed output.

_PWAIT = .F./.t.
Pauses between pages (if .T.).

_RMARGIN = *<expN>*
Page right margin (1 to 255).

_TABS = *<expC>*
Tab stops.

_WRAP = .F./.t.
Sets word wrapping between margins.

SQL COMMAND REFERENCE

The *Structured Query Language* (SQL) began in the mainframe and minicomputer environment. SQL is an advanced relational database language. The following commands are valid SQL commands:

ALTER TABLE *<table-name>* **ADD** (*<column-name><data-type>*[, *<column-name><data-type>*...]);
Adds new columns to an existing table.

CLOSE *<cursor-name>*;
Closes an SQL cursor.

CREATE DATABASE [*path*] *<datafile>*;
Creates an SQL database and set of SQL catalog tables for the new SQL datafile.

CREATE [UNIQUE] **INDEX** *<index-name>* **ON** *<table>* (*<column-name>* [ASC/DESC] [, *<column-name>*...]);
Creates an index based on one or more columns in a table or view.

CREATE SYNONYM *<synonym-name>* **FOR** *<table/view-name>*;
Defines an alternate name for a table or view.

CREATE TABLE <*table-name*> (<*column-name*><*data-type*> [, ...]);
Creates a new table, defining the columns within that table.

CREATE VIEW <*view-name*>[(<*column-name*>, <*column-name*>...)] **AS** <SELECT-*command*> [WITH CHECK OPTION];
Creates a virtual table based on the columns defined in [<*column-list*>], other tables, or views.

DBCHECK [<*table-name*>];
Verifies that SQL catalog tables contain current SQL tables.

DBDEFINE [<*.dbf-file*>];
Creates SQL catalog table entries for dBASE IV datafiles.

DECLARE <*cursor-name*> **CURSOR FOR** <SELECT *command*> [FOR UPDATE OF <*column-list*>/<ORDER BY *clause*>];
Defines a cursor and an associated **SELECT** command that specifies a result table for the cursor.

DELETE FROM <*table-name*> [<*alias-name*>] [<WHERE *clause*>];
Deletes specified rows from a table.

DELETE FROM <*table-name*> **WHERE CURRENT OF** <*cursor-name*>;
Deletes the row identified by the cursor.

DROP DATABASE <*datafile-name*>;
Deletes an SQL datafile and removes all datafiles and index files from directory.

DROP INDEX <*index-name*>;
Deletes an existing SQL index.

DROP SYNONYM <*synonym-name*>;
Deletes an SQL synonym name.

DROP TABLE <*table-name*>;
Deletes an SQL table.

DROP VIEW *<view-name>*;
Deletes an SQL view.

FETCH *<cursor-name>* INTO *<variable-list>*;
Advances the cursor pointer and copies the values of the selected row into dBASE IV memory variables.

GRANT ALL [PRIVILEGES]/*<privilege-list>* ON [TABLE] *<table-list>* TO PUBLIC/*<user-list>* [WITH GRANT OPTION];
Grants user-access privileges and update privileges of tables and views.

INSERT INTO *<table-name>* [(*<column-list>*)] <SELECT-*command*>;
Inserts rows in a table or updatable view.

INSERT INTO *<table-name>* [(*<column-list>*)] VALUES (*<value-list>*);
Inserts rows in a table or updatable view.

LOAD DATA FROM [*path*] *<file-name>* INTO TABLE *<table-name>* [[TYPE] SDF/DIF/WKS/ SYLK/FW2/RPD/DBASEII/DELIMITED [WITH BLANK/WITH *<delimiter>*]];
Imports data from a foreign file into an SQL table.

OPEN *<cursor-name>*;
Opens a cursor, executes the associated select command and positions the cursor before the first row in the result table.

REVOKE ALL [PRIVILEGES]/*<privileges-list>* ON [TABLE] *<table-list>* FROM PUBLIC/*<user-list>*;
Removes table access and update privileges.

ROLLBACK [WORK];
Restores a table to its previous contents prior to execution of commands in a **BEGIN TRANSACTION, END TRANSACTION** command set.

RUNSTATS [*<table-name>*];
Updates statistics in SQL catalog tables of the current datafile.

SELECT *<clause>* [INTO *<clause>*] FROM *<clause>* [WHERE *<clause>*] [GROUP BY *<clause>*] [HAVING *<clause>*] [UNION *subselect*] [ORDER BY *<clause>*/FOR UPDATE OF *<clause>*] [SAVE TO TEMP *<clause>*];
Retrieves data from tables or views.

SHOW DATABASE;
Displays information about SQL database files.

START DATABASE [*<database-name>*];
Activates an SQL datafile.

STOP DATABASE;
Deactivates the current active SQL datafile.

UNLOAD DATA TO [*path*] *<file-name>* **FROM TABLE** *<table-name>* [[TYPE] **SDF/DIF/WKS/SYLK/FW2/RPD/DBASEII/DELIMITED** [WITH BLANK/WITH *<delimiter>*]];
Exports data from an SQL table to a foreign file.

UPDATE *<table-name>/<view-name>* **SET** *<column-name>* = *<expression>*...[WHERE *<search-condition>*];
Changes column values in rows of a table or updatable view.

UPDATE *<table>* **SET** *<column-name>* = *<expression>*,... **WHERE CURRENT OF** *<cursor-name>*;
Changes column values in rows of a table or updatable view.

SQL Functions

The following SQL functions are available through dBASE IV:

AVG ([ALL/DISTINCT] *<column-name>*/ *<column-expression>*)
Computes the average value of a numeric column in selected rows.

COUNT ([*/DISTINCT] *<column-name>*)
Counts the number of selected rows in a query.

MAX ([ALL/DISTINCT]] *<column-expression>* /*<column-name>*)
Returns the maximum value found in specified columns.

MIN ([ALL/DISTINCT] *<column-name>*/ *<column-expression>*)
Returns the minimum value found in specified columns.

SUM ([ALL/DISTINCT] *<column-name>*/ *<column-expression>*
Sums the values of a numeric column in selected rows.

INDEX

A

activating
- debugger, 34-35
- screens, 8-9

adding,
- files to memo fields, 11-12
- records at ends of files, 9-10
- records to databases from arrays, 10-11

advancing printers, 50
Applications Generator, invoking, 27
arrays
- establishing memory variables, 35
- replacing data in records, 89

assigning names to menus, 37-38
averaging, *see* calculating

B

bar menus
- assigning names, 37-38
- defining pads, 37-38
- program modules, 19-20

binary files, loading into memory, 68
binary programs, removing from memory, 20
blanks, in fields and records, 14-15
BNL (Binary Named List) files, creating, 43-44
boxes, drawing, 6-7

C

calculating various sums, 18-19
changing
- environment settings, 100-105
- file names, 87-88
- files, 48-50
- programs, 70-71

characters, placing in type-ahead buffer, 65
clearing screen, 7-9
closing files, 22-23, 84
- *see also* quitting

codes, *see* program codes
colors, changing of screen areas, 6-7
commands
- !, *see* RUN
- */&&, *see* NOTE
- =, *see* STORE
- ?/?? (sending output to printers and files), 1-2

??? (sending output to printer), 2-3
@...CLEAR/SCROLL, 7
@...SAY/GET, 3-6
@...TO/FILL/CLEAR/SCROLL, 6-7
ACCEPT, 7-8
ACTIVATE MENU, *see* DEFINE MENU/DEFINE PAD
ACTIVATE POPUP, *see* DEFINE POPUP
ACTIVATE SCREEN, 8-9
ACTIVATE WINDOW, *see* DEFINE WINDOW
APPEND, 9-10
APPEND FROM, 10-11
APPEND MEMO, 11-12
ASSIST, 13
AVERAGE, *see* CALCULATE
BEGIN/END TRANSACTION, 13-14
BLANK, 14-15
BROWSE, 15-17
CALCULATE/AVERAGE/SUM, 18-19
CALL, 19-20
CANCEL, 20-21
CHANGE, *see* EDIT
CLEAR, 21-22
CLOSE, 22-23
COMPILE, 23-24
CONTINUE, *see* LOCATE
CONVERT, 24-25
COPY, 25-26
COUNT, *see* CALCULATE
CREATE APPLICATION, 27
CREATE FROM, 27-28
CREATE/MODIFY LABEL, 28-29
CREATE/MODIFY QUERY/VIEW, 29-30
CREATE/MODIFY REPORT, 30-31
CREATE/MODIFY SCREEN, 31-32
CREATE/MODIFY STRUCTURE, 32-33
DEACTIVATE MENU, *see* DEFINE MENU/DEFINE PAD
DEACTIVATE POPUP, *see* DEFINE POPUP
DEACTIVATE WINDOW, *see* DEFINE WINDOW
DEBUG, 34-35
DECLARE, 35
DEFINE BAR, *see* DEFINE POPUP
DEFINE BOX, 36
DEFINE MENU/DEFINE PAD, 37-38
DEFINE POPUP, 38-39
DEFINE WINDOW, 39-40
DELETE FILE, *see* ERASE
DELETE TAG, 42-43
DELETE/PACK, 41-42
DEXPORT, 43-44
DIR, 44-45
DISPLAY, *see* LIST
DO, 45-46
DO CASE/ENDCASE, 46-47
DO WHILE/ENDDO, 47-48
EDIT/CHANGE, 48-50

EJECT/EJECT PAGE, 50
ERASE, 51-52
executing
  at menus, 74-78
  at specific lines, 76-77
  on mouse click, 75
EXPORT, 52-53
FIND, 53-55
FUNCTION, 55
GO/GOTO, 56
HELP, 57
IF/ENDIF, 58
IMPORT, 59
INDEX/REINDEX, 60-61
INPUT, 61-62
INSERT, 62-63
JOIN, 63-64
KEYBOARD, 65
LABEL FORM, 65-66
LIST/DISPLAY, 66-67
LOAD, 68
LOCATE, 68-69
LOGOUT, 69-70
MODIFY APPLICATION, *see* CREATE APPLICATION
MODIFY COMMAND/FILE, 70-71
MODIFY LABEL, *see* CREATE/MODIFY LABEL
MODIFY QUERY/VIEW, *see* CREATE/MODIFY QUERY/VIEW
MODIFY REPORT, *see* CREATE/MODIFY REPORT
MODIFY SCREEN, *see* CREATE/MODIFY SCREEN
MODIFY STRUCTURE, *see* CREATE/MODIFY STRUCTURE
MOVE WINDOW, *see* DEFINE WINDOW
NOTE, 72
ON ERROR/ESCAPE/KEY, 73
ON EXIT BAR/MENU/PAD/POPUP, 74
ON MENU/POPUP, 74-75
ON MOUSE, 75
ON PAD, 75-76
ON PAGE, 76-77
ON READERROR, 77
ON SELECTION BAR, 77
ON SELECTION MENU, 78
ON SELECTION PAD, *see* DEFINE MENU/DEFINE PAD
ON SELECTION POPUP, *see* DEFINE POPUP
PACK, *see* DELETE
PARAMETERS, 79
PLAY MACRO, 79-80
PRINTJOB/ENDPRINTJOB, 80-81
PRIVATE/PUBLIC, 81-82
PROCEDURE, 82-83
PROTECT, 83-84
QUIT, 84
READ, 85
RECALL, 85-86
REINDEX, *see* INDEX

RELEASE, 86-87
RENAME, 87-88
repeated
performance, 97
REPLACE, 88-89
REPLACE FROM
ARRAY, 89
REPORT FORM, 90-91
RESET, 91-92
RESTORE, 92-93
RESUME, 93
RETRY, 93-94
RETURN, 94
ROLLBACK, 13-14
RUN/!, 95-96
SAVE, 96-97
SCAN/ENDSCAN, 97
SEEK, 98
SELECT, 99
SET, 100-105
SHOW MENU, *see*
DEFINE MENU
SHOW POPUP, *see*
DEFINE POPUP
SKIP, 105-106
SORT, 106-107
specified condition
sets, executing,
47-48
SQL (Structured
Query Language),
133-138
STORE, 107
SUM, *see* CALCULATE
SUSPEND, 108
TEXT, ENDTEXT,
108-109
TOTAL, 109-110
TYPE, 110
UNLOCK, 111
UPDATE, 111-112
USE, 112-113
WAIT, 113-114
ZAP, 114
compiling files, 23-24
conditional processing
of program
commands, 58
Control Center screen,
accessing, 13
control codes, printers,
2-3
controlling program flow
from specific
conditions, 46-47
converting file
structures, 24-25
copying
field data, 25-26
files, 25-26
files and file
structure, 25-26
files for other
applications, 52-53
indexes, 25-26
records, 25-26
correcting errors, 73
counting, *see* calculating
creating
Binary Named List
(BNL) files, 43-44
file structures, 27-28,
32-33
files from other
software, 59
indexes from
expressions or key
fields, 60-61
current record pointer,
moving, 105-106
current session,
closing, 84
cursors, positioning in
specified formats, 3-6

D

data
  changing
    in fields, 88-89
    in records, 88-89
  compiling into files, 23-24
  encrypting, 83-84
  entering, 61-62, 85
  error trapping during entry, 77
  keyboard entry, user prompting, 7-8
  passing with local variables, 79
  reading, 85
  replacing records data with array data, 89
  retrieving deleted, *see* recalling
  searching in indexed fields, 53-55
  securing, 83-84
  specified formats, 3-6
  storing entries to memory variables, 7-8
data-entry screens, designing and modifying, 31-32
database design screen, changing file structures, 32-33
dBASE IV functions, 115-126
debugging procedures and programs, 34-35
default settings, SET command, 100-105
defining
  bar and pop-up menu parameters, 37-39
  text boxes, 36
  user-defined functions (UDF), 55
  windows locations, parameters and sizes, 39-40
deleting
  files, 51-52
  records, 41-42, 85-86
designing
  labels, 28-29
  menus, 27
  reports, report design screen, 30-31
  see also generating
disks, deleting files from, 51-52
displaying
  directories of files, 44-45
  Help screen, 57
  on-screen information, 66-67
  records as tables, 15-17
  text files, 110
dot prompt, returning to, 20-21
drawing boxes, 6-7

E

editing
  files, 48-50
  keyboard shortcuts, 49-50
  see also changing
entering
  data, 61-62, 85
  see also reading
environment settings, changing, 100-105
erasing
  files from disk, 51-52
  screens, 21-22
  windows, 21-22

errors
  correcting or escaping, 73
  retrying commands, 93-94
  trapping, 77
executing
  commands
    at menus, 74-78
    at specific lines, 76-77
    in specified condition sets, 47-48
    with mouse, 75
  macros, 79-80
  programs, 45-46, 95-96
  suspended programs, *see* resuming
  see also running
exporting files, 52-53
extended structures, creating files from, 27-28

F

fields
  adding files, 11-12
  copying data, 25-26
  filling with blanks, 14-15
  numeric, totaling, 109-110
  searching for data, 53-55
  updating, 111-112
files
  adding
    fields, 24-25
    records at end, 9-10
    to a specific location, 62-63
    to databases and from arrays, 10-11
    to memo fields, 11-12
  binary, loading into memory, 68
  Binary Named List (BNL), creating, 43-44
  closing, 21-23, 84
  compiling, 23-24
  copying, 52-53
  creating
    from extended structures, 27-28
    from other software, 59
  deleting
    from disk, 51-52
    records, 41-42
  displaying
    directories, 44-45
    on-screen information, 66-67
    tables, 15-17
  editing, 48-50
  encrypting, 83-84
  erasing from disk, 51-52
  exporting, 52-53
  extensions for BNL files, 44
  importing, 59
  inserting notes, 72
  joining, 63-64
  label format file, printing labels, 65-66
  marking beginning and ending, 13-14
  merging, 63-64
  modifying in table format, 15-17

moving record pointer, 56
names, changing, 87-88
opening, 99, 112-113
printing, 90-91, 108-109
removing records, 41-42, 114
resetting integrity tags, 91-92
restoring, 13-14
searching for records, 68-69
securing, 83-84
sending output to, 1-2
single to multiuser access, 24-25
skipping back and forth within, 105-106
structures
changing, 24-25, 32-33
copying, 25-26
text displaying, 110
unlocking, 111
updating current, 111-112

financial calculating, 18-19
footers, printing, 51
formats, information display, 3-6
formatting output, 2
functions
dBASE IV, 115-126
Help screen, 57
low-level file I/O, 127-128
Structured Query Language (SQL), 133-138
user-defined, (UDF), 55

G

generating
labels, 27-29
menus, 27
reports, report design screen, 30-31
see also designing

H

headers, printing, 51
Help screen, displaying, 57

I

identifying subroutines, 82-83
importing files, 59
indexes
copying, 25-26
creating from expressions or key fields, 60-61
tags, removing from multiple index files, 42-43
updating, 61
inputting data, 61-62
inserting files and notes, 62-63, 72
integrity tags, resetting from files, 91-92

J

joining files and/or records, 63-64

K

keyboard entry of data, user prompting, 7-8

keyboard shortcuts
  Ctrl-End, 7-10, 33, 43, 61-63, 70, 100
  Ctrl-Q, 17
  Ctrl-U, 42, 86
  Esc, 17, 54-57
  F1, 34, 57
  F2, 19, 41, 54, 69, 86, 98, 106
  F3, 64
  F4, 64
  F5, 64
  F10, 56
  Q, 35
  Shift-F1, 19
  Shift-F2, 33, 43, 60, 106
  Shift-F4, 69
  Shift-F10, 80
  U, 35

L

label design screen
  starting, 28-29
label format files, 65-66
labels, printing, 65-66
loading binary files into memory, 68
local memory variables, private and public, 81-82
logging off current session, 69-70
low-level file I/O functions, 127-128

M

macros
  executing, 79-80
  saving to memory, 96-97
memo fields, adding files, 11-12
memory
  calling binary program modules, 19-20
  loading binary files, 68
  removing binary programs, 20
  removing contents, 86-87
  retrieving
    macros, 92-93
    memory variables, 92-93
    screen images, 92-93
    windows, 92-93
  saving data, 96-97
  variables
    creating, 107
    establishing, 35
    removing, 86-87
    saving, 96-97, 107
    storing entries, 7-8
    system, 129-131
menus
  designing, 27
  executing commands at exit, 74-78
  removing from memory, 86-87
merging files and records, 63-64
  see also joining
modifying
  programs, 70-71
  records in tables, 15-17
  reports, 30-31
mouse, executing commands, 75
moving
  current record pointer, 56, 105-106

printed pages, 51
specified areas of screen, 7

N

names of files, changing, 87-88
notes in files, 72
numeric fields, storing and totaling, 109-110

O

on-screen information, displaying, 1-2, 66-67
opening files, 112-113
output
  formatting, 2
  sending to files or printer, 1-3

P

passing data with local variables or parameters, 79
pausing programs, 113-114
placing characters in type-ahead buffer, 65
pop-up menus
  defining, 38-39
  removing from memory, 86-87
positioning active records, *see* sorting
positioning cursors, 3-6
printers
  advancing paper, 50
  control codes, 2-3
  moving to next page, 51
  sending output to, 1-3, 108-109
printing
  footers, 51
  headers, 51
  labels, 28-29, 65-66
  multiple copies, 80-81
  report files, 90-91
  reports (report design screen), 30-31
  starting and stopping, 80-81
  text boxes in reports, 36
  text to screens/ printers/files, 108-109
private memory variables, 81-82
processing conditional program commands, 58
program code, generating, 27
program flow, controlling from specific conditions, 46-47
program modules
  calling from memory, 19-20
  removing from memory, 86-87
programs
  changing, 70-71
  debugging, 34-35
  entering data, 61-62
  files, closing, 20-21
  modifying, 70-71
  pausing, 113-114
  processing conditional commands, 58
  restoring control, 94

resuming, 93, 137
running, 45-46, 95-96
stopping execution, 20-21
suspending execution, 108
writing, 70-71
public memory variables, 81-82

Q

query design screen, calculations and sorting, 29-30
quitting current session, 69-70
see also logging off

R

reading data, 85
recalling
deleted records, 85-86
macros, 92-93
memory variables, 92-93
screen images, 92-93
windows, 92-93
record pointer, moving, 56, 105-106
records
accessing, 17
adding
at specific location, 62-63
from arrays and databases, 10-11
to ends of files, 9-10
copying, 25-26
deleting from files, 41-42
displaying or modifying in tabular format, 15-17
filling with blanks, 14-15
joining, 63-64
recalling, 85-86
removing all files, 114, 136
searching, 68-69, 98
sorting, 106-107
updating fields, 111-112
releasing files for modifying, 111
removing
all records in files, 114
binary programs from memory, 20
files from specified disk, 51-52
index tags from multiple index files, 42-43
marked records from files, 41-42
memory contents, 86-87
repeating commands, 97
replacing data in records, 88-89
report design screen, designing and printing reports, 30-31
report files, printing, 90-91
reports, designing, modifying, and printing, 30-31
resetting integrity tags from files, 91-92

restoring
control to
programs, 94
files, 13-14
resuming suspended programs, 93, 137
retrieving, *see* recalling
retrying commands, 93-94
returning to dot prompt, 20-21
running
commands, 95-96
programs, 45-46, 95-96

S

saving to memory, 96-97
scanning commands in files, 97
screens
accessing Control Center, 13
activating, 8-9
clearing windows, 8-9
designing data formats, 31-32
displaying Help, 57, 66-67
erasing, 21-22
images, saving to memory, 96-97
moving sections to new areas, 7
printing text, 108-109
removing from memory, 86-87
scrolling windows, 8-9
specified areas, clearing and/or moving contents, 7
starting Edit screen, 48-50
scrolling windows from screen, 8-9
searching
fields, 53-55
files, 68-69, 98
securing data, 83-84
selection bars, executing commands, 77
SET command, default settings, 100-137
setting environments, 100-105
sorting active records, query design screen, 29-30, 106-107
specified condition sets, executing commands, 47-48
starting
existing files, forms design screen, 31-32
new screen from current session, 69-70
printing, 80-81
see also running
statistics, calculating, 18-19
stopping
printing, 80-81
program execution, 20-21
programs
temporarily, 108
storing
memory
variables, 107
numeric totals, 109-110
Structured Query Language (SQL) commands and functions, 133-138

structures of files, changing, 32-33
subroutines, identifying, 82-83
suspending program execution, 108
system memory variables, 129-131
systems, securing, 83-84

T

tables, records displaying or modifying, 15-17
tags, removing from multiple index files, 42-43
text
- boxes, defining, 36
- files, displaying type, 110
- printing to files, screens, and printers, 108-109

transactions, marking start and end, 13-14
trapping errors, 77
type-ahead buffer
- clearing, 21-22
- placing characters, 65

U

unlocking files, *see* releasing
updating
- current files or fields, 111-112
- indexes, 61

user-defined functions (UDF), 55

W

waiting, *see* pausing
windows
- clearing or scrolling from screen, 8-9
- defining parameters, 39-40
- erasing, 21-22
- removing from memory, 86-87
- saving to memory, 96-97

writing programs, 70-71

Z

zapping all records in files, 114